BEHIND THE MASK OF
TUTANKHAMEN

Portrait of a studious and dedicated archaeologist who's tenacity over a quarter of a century gave the world a unique insight into the cradle of Western civilisation – the tomb of Tutankhamen.

BEHIND THE
MASK OF
TUTANKHAMEN

Barry Wynne

SOUVENIR PRESS

Printed in Great Britain by
Clarke, Doble & Brendon Ltd
Plymouth

CONTENTS

To the memory of my Father,
To the present of my darling Wife,
To the future of my Sons
This book is dedicated.

ILLUSTRATIONS

9

Telegrams} Highclere 204.
Telephone}

*Many books have been written on the subject of my father's
friendship and long-standing support of Howard Carter, in
his effort to discover the tomb of Tutankhamen.*

*The story is not an easy one to tell, owing to the fact
that most of my family papers were destroyed in a blitz
on London in the Second World War.   Also, as I understand
it, few records remain at the Cairo Museum.   However, at
the request of the author, I have done my best, at this
long remove of time, to give him as much factual assistance
that I could establish.   Furthermore, it is only too true
that 'old men forget'.*

*Nevertheless, it has been a pleasure to assist such a
dedicated man as Mr. Barry Wynne has proved himself to be
and, if I have in any way helped to establish a firsthand
documentary record for posterity, then I, for one, will be
more than delighted.*

ACKNOWLEDGEMENTS

THE Author wishes to acknowledge the following with his most grateful thanks:

The Rt. Hon. Sixth Earl of Carnarvon, *The Times* newspapers, the authors and publishers of almost every book written on the subject of Tutankhamen, all of which were consulted for reference, including Howard Carter's original works, now available in a paperback edition, published by Sphere. Also he wishes to thank His Excellency, the Minister of Egyptian Tourism, Ibrahim Neguib, the Under-Secretary of State for Tourism, Adel Taher, and my good friend, Samir Raouf; also Kamall el Mallakh, El Ahram. Finally, but not least, John Rose, who conceived the idea, and R. A. Ferrao, who has been most helpful.

Photographs: Times Newspapers Ltd.,
The Griffith Institute, Oxford.

INTRODUCTION

THIS book has not been conceived for the shelf of the academic, neither is it an everyman's guide to Egyptology.

Rather is it the story told in human terms of the premature death of a young boy-king who was confined to his eternal resting place over three thousand years ago, only to be disturbed in his tranquil sleep by a small, but resolute, band of English archaeologists thirsting for new insight into the cradle of western civilisation.

Of these latter, each were individuals motivated from differing walks of life, but all intent on contributing to the sum total of historic record. Each was prey to his own peculiarity of character and it is the interplay of these personalities to the extraordinary circumstances of the time that add drama and unbridled excitement to this unique 'dig' at Luxor.

That the story has become interlaced with a legend of the effect of the supernatural upon the lives of some of these men is a matter of public record. How much credence can be placed on these sometimes bizarre, if uncanny events must rest with the reader. The author would only like to add that he has based the story on considerable first-hand evidence, but has also drawn widely on other published and unpublished material. This he gratefully acknowledges.

CHAPTER ONE

THE BREATHLESS SCENE

HOWARD CARTER was in solemn mood. His mount shook its head for the thousandth time, in an effort to dislodge the pestilential flies, as they walked the last few yards to the edge of the western bank of the Nile opposite Luxor. When a glance from the back of his donkey informed him that both Thomas Cook ferryboats were moored on the opposite shore, he could not withhold yet another sigh. He would have to bear the delay with patience. This, at least, he had learned after thirty years spent in Egypt.

But even as Carter gazed in some frustration across the burnished surface of the water, molten red, tinged with blues and green, his spirits began to rise as ever they did when the graceful columns of the Temple of Luxor were caught and gilded by the slanting rays of the setting sun. They became transmuted, restored to life and beauty. Such a breathless scene was his inspiration and nurtured within him the dedication to seek ever more knowledge of those ancient Egyptians who had created the wonderful Necropolis of Thebes, one-time capital of Upper and Lower Egypt.

A beturbaned fellahin reluctantly climbed from the shade of a tree, walked to the water's edge, leaned far out, as if that would help him, and, cupping his hands, let out a long, piercing cry, a cross between a muezzin's call to prayer and the agonised outpourings of a tormented soul in Hell. It echoed across the river and seemed just likely to reach the far side. It was a still

evening, comparatively cool after the recent heat of summer. The month was October; the year 1922.

Howard Carter was forty-nine years old. He had been born in Swaffham, Norfolk, and was the son of a talented animal painter. Of medium height, dapper, and average build, he had bushy, dark eyebrows and a generous but neat moustache. He brooked no concession in his wardrobe to the climate of the region. Dressed in a three-piece suit, sporting a bow-tie, pocket-handkerchief and a Homburg hat, he would not have been out of place on the sidewalk of any European capital. He had endured frail health as a child, which had left its mark in his somewhat taciturn nature.

He had travelled to Cairo at a youthful seventeen, joining the

The location of the Pharaoh Tutank-hamen's tomb in the Valley of the Kings, shortly after discovery. An estimated two hundred thousand tons of rock chipping had been removed by hand under the supervision of Howard Carter. The task took ten years.

Photo: 'The Times'

staff of the Egyptian Exploration Fund Archaeological Survey as a draughtsman. Even his early career was to be crowned with considerable achievement. After many years of faithful service he had been appointed Inspector-General of the Antiquity Department of the Egyptian Government. In this position he reorganised the antiquity administration of Upper Egypt under Sir William Garstin and Sir Gaston Maspero, but in those days, as in present times, archaeology was hampered by lack of funds.

However, by great good fortune, during the winter of 1902–3 the Upper Nile area was visited by an American tourist, Theodore M. Davis, a lawyer of Newport, Rhode Island. He was entranced by what he found.

It was explained to him that, during the three thousand millennia before Christ, some thirty dynasties of Pharaohs, encompassed within the Old Kingdom, the Middle Kingdom and the New Kingdom, had ruled Ancient Egypt. Further that the tombs of some sixty or seventy of the three hundred and twenty Pharaohs had already been found, but that a short gap in the Eighteenth Dynasty was tantalising modern archaeologists. The American was intrigued and decided to offer to finance the Department of Antiquities to further explore Bibân-el-Malûk, more popularly known as the Valley of the Tombs of the Kings, on the western bank of the Nile at Luxor. Within the valley dozens of tombs had already been found; Davis now determined to complete the historic record and demanded no financial compensation in return.

In the following season Howard Carter began work for him and, while under his patronage, was eventually to discover the tomb of Thothmes IV. In the following year the expedition found six other important and inscribed tombs: those of Queen Hatshepsût, Yuaa and Tuaa, King Siptah, Prince Mentuherkhepshef, the heretic King Akhenaton and King Horemheb. In one unnamed tomb they discovered the beautiful gold jewellery of Queen Tausret.

In fact it was during these early expeditions in the valley that objects were first discovered bearing the name Tutankhamen. But it was in 1906 that an Englishman, Edward Ayrton, found, under a large tilted rock, a beautiful blue glazed cup, bearing a cartouche of Tutankhamen. However, it was Herbert Winlock, of the New York Metropolitan Museum – who was to play such a major role in the months to come – who positively identified the seals on the lids of several jars and the cartouche on the porcelain goblet as being those of a pharaoh, King Tutankhamen. The following year a rock-cut chamber was found and it contained so many objects bearing the king's name that Theodore Davis was convinced that this must be Tutankhamen's tomb. Believing that he had now found all, Davis relinquished his concession and returned to America. Howard Carter was convinced to the opposite view.

He was determined to proceed, believing vehemently that they had not yet found the tomb.

This decision coincided with two unrelated events which were to have a profound effect upon his life. The first was a disagreement with his employers, which forced him to resign, and the second a car accident in Germany, which seriously injured the fifth earl of Carnarvon.

Lord Carnarvon was a keen, early motorist and was driving south through Germany with his chauffeur, Edward Trotman, when, on a straight stretch of road near Bad Langenschwalb, his lordship breasted a short incline in the road to find two bullock wagons intent on passing one another. Lord Carnarvon, who was driving at the time, swerved violently and pitched the car into a ditch. He had been on his way to join his wife, the Countess Almina, on the French Riviera.

Trotman was hurled out into a pinewood, but fortunately escaped serious injury. Coming to, he raced to the overturned car to find his master pinned beneath the vehicle, being asphyxiated by the soft mud at the ditch's bottom. Scooping it away, he shouted frantically to some farm labourers to assist him and, in due time, managed to extricate his lordship from the wreckage. Never a strong man, Lord Carnarvon's injuries affected his chest and he was advised thereafter to winter abroad.

It was while convalescing in Egypt that the earl, always an active man, consulted the British Representative, Lord Cromer, seeking his advice as to how to pass his time profitably. The latter immediately suggested archaeology but, upon his lordship professing no knowledge of this fascinating subject – although he was a keen collector of antiques – Lord Cromer said that this was no obstacle as an erudite Englishman, by name Howard Carter, could be employed privately to assist and advise him. He promised to effect an introduction. The two men met, took to one another and Carter was immediately offered a contract at £400 per annum, being a third more than he was presently earning.

Lord Carnarvon then negotiated with the Egyptian government to take over Theodore Davis's concession to dig in the valley. To compensate his financial investment a clause in the licence permitted Lord Carnarvon the right to sell or retain duplicate objects so long as they were not 'unique' and, providing also that they did not come from an 'unpillaged' tomb, in which case all treasures and articles must remain the property of the Egyptian government.

This provision at least allowed Howard Carter the opportunity of selling certain items to museums and collectors around the world, from which source he was able, on behalf of his patron, to reimburse some small part of the overall investment.

These negotiations had taken place some thirteen years previously in 1909.

Carter's present melancholic mood had its origins in the realisation that he was now almost at the very end of his long excavation of the Valley of the Kings, which he had been conducting for ten years on behalf of his benefactor and long-time friend, the Earl of Carnarvon. Their concession to dig from the Egyptian government was due to expire in just ten days time; he was now examining the final few feet of ground.

Their unremitting search for what was believed to be the last undiscovered tomb of a pharaoh in the valley had encompassed a decade. As he contemplated the situation, musing on the staggering fact that they had just completed the movement, by hand, of some estimated 200,000 tons of sand and rubble, he acknowledged to himself that, after all, ten years was but a ripple in the history of the Nile, however significant it might be in their own lifespan. It mattered not that during this period their country had endured a blood-letting war, sacrificing the flower of its youth; here it made no difference. The sun still rose and set over Luxor with little visible change, as it had for thousands of years. During the war their excavations had been suspended, but having resumed at the earliest opportunity, another four years had passed, yet nothing had they found.

Carter suddenly became aware that the ferrymen had acknowledged his presence and were already nosing their craft into mid-stream. He sat idly watching its progress as the sturdy engine drove the vessel swiftly across the current.

Carter watched the bowman lasso the post on the quayhead; only two passengers disembarked. He walked down the short ramp, muttered a somewhat less than generous greeting and sat down upon the cushioned seats beneath the awning. A few local villagers followed him and after a brief interval the ferry cast off and the Egyptian helmsman pointed her bow in the direction of the quay beneath the Winter Palace Hotel.

The sun had departed, leaving but a hazy afterglow which bathed the opposite shore in softest light. Palm trees stood motionless, their fronds etched against the backdrop sky. Two dhows made silent and majestic passage across the dark surface of the water, while an assortment of other craft clung closely to the banks. All was still. A pale half-moon had risen behind the Mosque of Sidi Habou'l-Haggag, her presence, as yet unfulfilled, following too closely upon the departure of her rival.

Howard Carter wondered idly whether Lord Carnarvon had caught his train that morning. It had been a sombre dinner the previous evening. Carter's last request of his lordship, before their concession and partnership should end, reflected not only his personal integrity but also his professional dedication to completing a task in hand. He was determined that in those last few days remaining, having covered the entire Valley of the Kings metre by metre, stone by stone, that he would culminate the operation by removing a thirty-foot mound of chippings and debris right within their camp and only a few feet from the entrance to the long-discovered tomb of Rameses VI. In fact the rubble comprised ancient extract from the original excavators of the tomb. With all their remaining equipment packed and ready for removal, he had left but six men to complete this task. Lord Carnarvon had generously agreed, and upon that sad note the two men had parted.

Carnarvon, who was only making a flying visit to Cairo, having deviated from a journey to Salonika, was accompanied on this visit by his half-brother, Mervyn Herbert. He had decided to return to Cairo and England the following day. Carter had not yet mentally adjusted himself to the fact that shortly he would be out of work. There had been talk of another concession, but he was not a man to contemplate the future until the present had been resolved.

A bat slipped out from the approaching bank, darting and diving in its search for prey. The engine was thrust into reverse, causing the ferry to tremble and gush turmoil at its stern. A thud indicated that they had made contact with the quay and Carter awoke from his reverie. He climbed the steps, oblivious to the bustling life around him.

Even at this very moment the day express from Cairo had just come to a grinding halt at Luxor Station, amidst columns of smoke and hissing steam. The weary travellers disgorged from their open-sided carriages, a seething, shouting, odorous mass of people. Also on to the platform stepped a young English military policeman, tall, well-built and singularly out of place amidst the cacophony of the local populace. His shoulders and red capband stood out like a beacon as he made his way to the exit and inquired directions to the Winter Palace Hotel. He broke from the confusion of the station to the comparative security of the street. He was immediately alive to the sights and sounds of this country town in Upper Egypt, something over four hundred and fifty miles south of the modern capital. He liked what he saw and was glad to exercise his blood-starved limbs.

Recently promoted sergeant, Richard Adamson decided to walk rather than take a carriage. He was a Yorkshireman, aged twenty-five, and had been stationed in Egypt for some three years. This first visit to Luxor was to his liking, for it made a break from routine. However, as is common practice in the

British Army, he had been the last to be informed of the reason for his temporary detachment to 'the staff of Lord Carnarvon'. Son of a wholesale tailor in Leeds, an ex-infantryman in the Duke of Wellington's who had seen bloody action in France, he had since transferred to the Military Police. He was blessed, or cursed, by the outspokenness of a Yorkshireman, only somewhat restrained after years of military discipline. He also had a natural diffidence which singled him out for those 'special duties' so beloved of authority.

His outgoing and casual approach to life often led him into bizarre situations. This could be no better exemplified than when he arrived in France. Within four hours of disembarkation his unit filed into their place in the trenches, being told to take care to walk round the dead German soldier who was slumped against the sandbags of the re-occupied trench. Casually, Adamson popped up on to the top of the parapet to avoid him, oblivious of his mortal danger. A rattle of oaths and curses erupted from around his feet and inclined him to take cover before an astonished or lethargic enemy had fortunately had time to react. He admitted that his training had been so scanty that he did not know how to fire his rifle. This deficiency was very shortly remedied.

At the cessation of hostilities the Duke of Wellingtons' travelled south to Marseilles, *en route* to Gibraltar, where three weeks later they boarded a trooper destined for Constantinople. It was even as they began to approach that Levantine city that political trouble flared in Egypt. Word went round that volunteers were immediately required to boost the ranks of the Military Police in Cairo. Adamson found himself an impressed volunteer. Belligerently inquiring how long he would be required, he was enlightened by his sergeant with the use of a solitary word: 'Permanent.' Dutifully he signed on for four years with the Colours and was promoted corporal for his pains.

After three weeks in Constantinople – CONSTANT to the British soldiery – he received orders to embark once more, this time for Port Said. Upon arrival they immediately journeyed to

Bab-el-Hadid Barracks, near the railway station in Cairo. They arrived at precisely fifteen minutes before noon. At two p.m. a somewhat bemused, if not disgruntled Military Policeman, he was marching out on his first and lone patrol. The rough-and-ready, pugilistic provost sergeant had told him to walk in the middle of the road, to avoid trouble, and to meet him at a patrol point two hours later. Well schooled, after years of experience with British non-commissioned officers, Adamson made no protest. As the moment for rendezvous drew near he had to admit to himself that he was irretrievably lost. It seemed to him that it would offend his sense of the ridiculous to inquire of the local population his present whereabouts and also directions to the point at which he was to make contact with his sergeant. There was nothing else he could do but keep impressively on the march. Some hours later a searching patrol duly regained possession of their latest recruit.

It was not long before the newcomer to the ranks of the Military Police realised that the policeman's lot was not a happy one, especially in Cairo, 1919. Lurid stories were rife as to what they might expect if they were to stray alone into certain districts, principally the red light area of Mouski. Before going out on patrol the following day, four strong, with drawn revolvers, they were warned yet again not to stray from their route of patrol. Adamson, not content with this simple instruction from his superior, inquired whether anyone had ever been lost before. 'Two or three,' was the sardonic rejoinder. 'And what happened to them?' the innocent asked. 'Never been seen again,' was the laconic reply.

Whether or not it was the intention of the British authorities to put fear into the heart of the local populace, certainly the provost sergeant put the fear of God into the hearts of his men. Friday nights were worst when the troops stationed in Cairo, both British and Indian, received their pay. Each Friday at 9.30 p.m. exactly, the combined forces of the Military Police, both foot and mounted patrols, entered the brothel areas to ferret out the troops from their romantic assignations. The confusion was indescribable; bottles and knives were used in the high pitched battles, both inside the houses and on the streets. Even the girls joined in. More often than not the Indian soldiers climbed on to the rooftops. Many a time Adamson found himself clinging for dear life to a parapet in his attempt to dislodge a reluctant sepoy.

At the height of the tumult, when matters were becoming fast out of hand, a line of mounted policemen would string out across the top of the street. Between the two outside horsemen a light chain would be attached, curving down behind them, lying loose on the ground. At a command the men would spur their horses. The charge would clear all before it and the 'blood wagons' would be filled with prisoners for transfer to the military and civil gaols. This activity did not appeal to Corporal Adamson.

However, some of his duties were peaceful. On one particular day he had an encounter of a different order. He was checking credentials on the wooden bridge that spanned the Suez Canal, standing on the Kantara side. A party of twelve men, led by a venerable gentleman, with a large black hat and long beard, crossed the bridge and proffered his civilian pass. Their destination was Palestine. Adamson glanced down at the papers and, as he looked up, caught the penetrating gaze of the leader of the party.

'Yes, sir, these seem to be in order; you may pass.'

With the faintest of smiles the man replied softly : 'We have been waiting two thousand years to hear those words.'

'What do you mean?' the soldier inquired.

'Never mind,' came the serene reply.

After they had passed Adamson turned to an Egyptian policeman : 'Who was that then?'

'Dr Weizmann, the Jewish leader,' his colleague replied.

Three weeks later, for no specified reason, Richard Adamson found himself transferred to the Military Police Staff at the British Embassy. This was to remain his post, on and off, for three long years. Field-Marshal Lord Allenby was the High

Commissioner and Commander-in-Chief Egypt, and it was not long before the corporal made his acquaintance. He was respected, indeed highly regarded by British troops of every rank. Yet he was a strict disciplinarian.

One morning Lord Allenby, walking out of the embassy, noticed two private soldiers who passed him without saluting. He did not refer to the group of officers walking at his side, but turned to a sentry: 'Fetch those two men.'

With alacrity the man obeyed and shortly the two offenders were standing as if turned to stone before their Commander-in-Chief.

'You saw that I was an officer, why did you not salute?'

There was a brief silence until one of the luckless men managed to stammer: 'We . . . we thought you had passed us, sir, and that you hadn't seen.'

'That is no explanation; you always salute an officer of whatever rank. Do not let it happen again.'

Suitably chastened the men were dismissed at the double.

It was also well known among the troops that Lady Allenby was constantly inspecting kitchens, messing halls, hospitals in an attempt to raise the standard of their welfare.

During the next few years at the embassy Adamson was frequently to see Lord Carnarvon, but he never exchanged more than a polite, 'Good morning, my lord.' Howard Carter had also been a visitor, but Adamson did not remember him.

Life was pleasant enough in Cairo, although increasingly punctuated by hostile demonstrations, as the Egyptian people became ever more determined to throw off the yoke of British colonial rule. Suddenly matters took a distinct turn for the worse when a young Egyptian student, Hassenein Ali, a member of the Wafd Party, hurled a grenade at the then Prime Minister, Nessim Pasha. In fact he made a mistake, believing him to be Sir Lee Stack, Sirdar of the Egyptian Army and the Governor of the Sudan. The attempt proved abortive and the student was caught. Tried by military tribunal before General Lawson, he was convicted and hanged. Adamson was detailed to attend the execution, having acted as the accused's escort throughout the trial. The experience affected him for life. The corporal gained so much information from the student during the trial that the Cairo Police Chief, Russell Pasha, was able to issue warrants for the arrest of all the leading members of the Wafd Party.

At the 'Cairo Conspiracy Trial' that followed, the main defendant was Nationalist Opposition Leader, Abdul Rhaman Fahy Bey, who was defended by the English counsel, Mitchel Innes, K.C. Just prior to the opening of proceedings a threat was made on the life of the President of the Court, General Lawson. Corporal Adamson was immediately ordered to become his personal bodyguard, sitting on the Bench beside the judge and accompanying him everywhere he went.

At the end of the long trial Fahy Bey and twenty-seven other defendants were found guilty and their leader was sentenced to death. In fact, he boasted to Adamson that the British would never dare hang him and such turned out to be the case. When Adamson accompanied the President of the Court back to his hotel for the last time, the general suddenly made a suggestion : 'Corporal, I think it might be a good idea if you were to be posted away from Cairo for a short time. Perhaps your face is rather too familiar for safety.'

'As a matter of fact, sir,' the corporal answered diffidently, 'I had been thinking the selfsame thing.'

Two days later his name went up on 'Orders'.

CORPORAL R. ADAMSON PROMOTED TO THE RANK OF ACTING SERGEANT AND TO PROCEED IMMEDI-ATELY TO LUXOR TO REPORT TO MR HOWARD CARTER, c/o LORD CARNARVON'S EXPEDITION, WINTER PALACE HOTEL.

What on earth was all this about? Station Sergeant Bloxham, to whom the corporal applied for information, gave the army's traditionally limited reply : 'No idea. You've got to pick up some survey equipment the army loaned his lordship's expedition. Your movement order will be ready in an hour or two; also your railway warrant. Cheer up, soldier, you may find yourself digging for buried treasure.'

Little did he know.

Corporal Adamson gripped his holdall firmly and walked into the refined atmosphere of the Winter Palace Hotel. In the spacious foyer, ceiling fans barely disturbed the still, cool air. By now used to the rarefied atmosphere of the British Embassy the Yorkshireman did not feel at all self-conscious as he looked for someone in command. He spotted an Egyptian manager.

'I've come to see Lord Carnarvon, or Mr Howard Carter.'

'I doubt if you'll be able to see them tonight,' the obsequious manager replied, casting his eye over the travel-stained soldier. 'We have a room booked for you at the back.'

A boy whisked away his holdall and Adamson meekly followed. The bedroom allocated was one retained for unexpected guests, but it was pleasant and airy. As the evening advanced the newly-fledged sergeant puzzled over the words of the manager, who seemed to indicate that he would be unable to meet his new masters until morning. Taking his courage in both hands he decided to explore.

The hotel was by no means full, for the tourist season was just about to begin. A number of foreigners were in residence; Germans, Swedes, French, Italians and British. It was not long before he managed to get into conversation and secure a drink for himself.

Some time later he decided to investigate still further the outlying rooms and found himself in a spacious lounge. Among several knots of people, one man sat alone, obviously an Englishman. Adamson decided to approach him.

'Excuse me, sir, I wonder if by any chance you happen to know Lord Carnarvon?'

The gentleman looked up and smiled.

Richard Adamson, Lance Corporal, at Gibraltar *en route* to Egypt immediately following the Armistice of the First World War.

'Indeed I do. He happens to be my half-brother. Who, may I ask, are you?'

'My name is Adamson, S'eant Adamson, sir. I've been sent down from Cairo.'

'Oh, I see,' the Honourable Mervyn Herbert replied. 'Then you had better come along with me. I think my brother is in the Smoking Room with one or two of his friends.'

The military policeman was mightily relieved.

'I'm very glad he is here, sir. I was beginning to wonder whether I'd ever find him.'

A few minutes later he was being introduced to his lordship, whom he immediately recognised from his visits to the embassy.

'Good evening, m'lord; Sergeant Adamson. I was told to report to you or a Mr Howard Carter.'

Lord Carnarvon looked up and smiled wanly. 'I didn't expect you so soon. Have you had anything to eat?'

'Indeed I have, sir, thank you.'

'Very good,' was the perfunctory reply. 'Then see Mr Carter in the morning. My brother will arrange anything you need.'

Blessed with this modicum of information it was clear that the conversation had ended and Adamson retired from the scene. With a rising sense of curiosity he decided to wander out for a stroll. He walked down the short drive, across the road lined with horses and traps, their oil lamps aglow, until he reached the eastern bank of the Nile. He managed to dismiss the few more stubborn peddlers who were pestering him with their mass-produced relics of the tombs, until finally he stood alone at the water's edge.

The moon was now high overhead, inducing a mood of romance and nostalgia. A steamer slipped by, lights ablaze, with the sound of music drifting on the still, warm air. Suddenly, Adamson heard the soft shuffle of someone approaching. Schooled to the disciplines of the metropolis he spun round.

'Good evening, sir,' a benign old man bade him.

He spoke well and Adamson imagined him to be a guide. He duly acknowledged the greeting. There was a marked difference between the people of Luxor and the city of Cairo, he had already noted. Here they were more gentle and dignified, as is so often the case with pastoral people. The old man squatted and the khaki-clad figure beside him returned his gaze to the distant shore.

'It is truly beautiful,' the voice murmured beside him, betraying his excellent command of English. There was silence for a time between the two men.

'Are you familiar with the legend of the Nile?'

There was nothing subservient in the question or ingratiating. Adamson felt a tinge of shame when he admitted that he did not, for Cairo was also on the banks of the Nile, and he had lived there for three long years. The old man annunciated his words with meticulous precision and they had the gentlest quality about them. The Englishman had little imagination but his interest was stirred.

'What legend?'

'Well, sir, you have to understand that if it were not for the Nile our country would be an immense desert, scorched into dust by a flaming sun, for without the river there would be no trees, vegetation or towns. Our ancient ancestors, therefore, considered the Nile to be one of their gods. They called him Hapi and he was father of the gods, master of the element who gave food to Egypt and, by flooding the country with his life-blood, ensured propagation.

'They believed that Hapi lived in a cave and came out at floodtime. Therefore at the summer solstice, when the fresh, clear waters came down from the chasms of Syene to Silsileh, the pharaoh and his priests conducted a great ceremony, sacrificing a bull and geese. Then they would throw into the water a roll of sealed papyrus containing their prayer that the country would gain the benefit of a good and normal flood. For you see, sir, a small flood would bring no benefit and a large flood could bring disaster. The peasants from far and wide would flock to the river to banquet and carouse for many a day. The priests would venture forth from the sanctuary of their temples in long processions and carry the statue of the god, Hapi, along the banks of the Nile, to the sound of music and chanting. Then from the coffers of their treasury they would pluck gold trinkets and precious stones, hurling them far out into the river in order that Hapi would be appeased and bring abundance to the inhabitants of the Nile Valley.

'Then, during the first days of June, the most beautiful virgin who could be found throughout Upper and Lower Egypt would be brought to the priests on the bank of the Nile. Here she would be bathed, anointed with perfume and oil, dressed in a scarlet silk robe and her hair crowned with a garland of flowers and covered with precious jewels. Then her hands and feet would be bound in chains. Next the priests would wrap her in a long veil of pure white silk and she would be carried to a boat painted in bright colours, decked with banners and multi-coloured lamps, upon which she would board to the sound of fifes and tambourines.

'The priests would then set sail to the confluence of the two branches of the Nile at the Delta. Around her neck, this virgin of sixteen, in her nuptial gown, would bear two inscriptions; one signified her parents' consent to her sacrifice; the other the governor's edict confirming her sentence.

'The priests then circled three times around the bride and, at the third turn, the victim was plunged into the river. Although usually totally overcome with terror, it was incumbent upon the child not to utter a sound before she sank beneath the water. Were she to cry out the incensed Hapi would not send the life-saving water and famine would fall upon the land. With such a penalty what proud girl would dare to bring such misfortune upon her people?'

By this time Adamson was watching intently the features of the speaker. The man seemed lost in the recounting of the legend. He paused, then turned with a sad smile. 'The origin of this story derives from a tale recorded by Plutarch and was retold by the Romans, then later by the Arabs. According to his account King Egyptos, ruler of Egypt, offered his own daughter as a supreme sacrifice to appease the furies of the gods at a time of famine. Having done so he was overcome by remorse and threw himself beneath the waters.

'These celebrations still survive to our present day and, each year, during the month of August, Egypt celebrates the sacrifice to the Nile flood. We call the custom Wafa-el-Nil, with the only difference being that the virgin has been replaced by a dummy.'

As if coming back to reality the old man concluded his story on an anti-climatic note. 'Actually there is not a single hieroglyphic inscription to confirm the fact that our ancient forefathers ever made such a human sacrifice,' he said, somewhat apologetically.

Adamson didn't really know quite what to say. He looked up at the moon poised in the midnight sky. Here anything seemed possible. 'Thank you for telling me the story,' the Yorkshireman murmured, and wondered if the man would expect any baksheesh. To his delighted surprise the storyteller simply rose to his feet, smiled a 'Good-night' and said : 'I trust you will enjoy your visit to Luxor, sir.'

CHAPTER TWO

VALLEY OF THE DEAD

HAVING arranged an early call, Adamson was up shortly after
the sun had tipped the horizon. He watched it for a few minutes
as it flooded with light the garden behind the hotel. In it grew
tall trees of many varieties. Atop their trunks birds chattered in
delighted expectation. A network of paths criss-crossed the
ground and, already, workmen were silently dowsing them
down with water. Dressed in white they looked like wraiths
moving in slow motion around the boles of the trees. As custom
demanded the sergeant attended his uniform, polishing his brass
and cleaning his shoes.

He went to the dining-room for breakfast and fed well. It
was when standing in idle contemplation in the foyer that the
message was given him.

'Please, sir, Mr Howard Carter would like to see you in the
garden.'

Rudely brought back to reality he hurried as bidden. Only
one couple sat on chairs beneath the trees and this was obviously
his man. He walked up smartly.

'Mr Carter, sir?' It could only be him.

'Yes. Good morning, eh . . .'

'S'eant Adamson, sir, from Cairo.'

'Yes, very good to see you. Did you sleep well?'

'Indeed I did, sir, thank you.'

'Excuse me, Howard, I'll see you later,' his young lady companion said, and disappeared.

'Sit down, Adamson.'

'Thank you, sir. By the way, Mr Carter, I saw Lord Carnarvon yesterday.'

'Did you indeed. When was that?' The man seemed surprised.

'Last evening, sir, after I arrived.'

'You were lucky then; he left for Cairo first thing this morning.'

Adamson's eyes opened in surprise.

'Left, sir . . . ?'

'Yes, he left us this morning. He's finished with us now. He only came down for a day from Cairo to tidy up his business.'

'But . . . but . . .'

Howard Carter broke in. 'You were lucky to see him. I only had an hour with him myself. His interest in this excavation is over. We have virtually completed our task. He is *en route* to England. In fact, this was only a very short visit. He has been travelling in Greece.'

Adamson was simply nonplussed, his blue eyes wide with surprise. For a moment there was a pause. Then Carter asked him: 'Don't you know why you have been sent down here?'

'No, sir, not really. We never know anything in the army until it's happening.'

Carter grunted. 'Bureaucracy is the same the world over.'

He changed the subject.

'Lord Carnarvon and I have been conducting a dig in the Valley of the Kings; we have almost finished and we are now packing up. The army kindly loaned us some survey equipment. Your job is to come across with me to the valley, check it against the inventory and then arrange to take it back by boat to Cairo.'

'Me, sir?' Adamson said in some astonishment.

'Yes, you,' countered Carter, with a touch of asperity. 'Now are you ready?'

'Yes, sir,' Adamson stuttered. 'My holdall is in the hall.'

But, as the sergeant climbed to his feet, he couldn't help addressing this neatly dressed Englishman yet once again. Certainly he looked like no archaeologist he had ever seen and he had watched plenty of them digging beside the Pyramids.

'Sir . . . ,' he began with temerity. 'I can't understand it. I was told that I would be joining the staff of Lord Carnarvon.'

Somewhat surprisingly, Carter was patient. 'Well, as I have explained to you, my dear man, Lord Carnarvon has finished with archaeology. We have completed our search of the valley . . . or almost so,' he enjoined, for the sake of accuracy. 'In a few days' time you will be able to take your equipment back to Cairo.'

'But I don't wish to go back to Cairo,' Adamson responded plaintively.

Carter, who had begun to move away, stopped in his tracks. 'Why on earth not?'

'Well, sir, it's a long story, but the authorities thought I should leave the city because I have been in the middle of all this political trouble . . . the Conspiracy Trial,' he added.

Carter decided to ignore him. 'Collect your bag, we must get down to the ferry.'

They walked along the drive in silence, crossed the road, descended the long flight of steps and found the vessel awaiting them. They stepped on board. Within five minutes they had cast off and for the first time Adamson saw the long range of sandy, white hills that blotted out the horizon on the far side of the river. They looked desolate and sunbaked. He began to wonder to where he was going. Carter caught his gaze. 'Deir-el-Bahri,' he said, attuned to the soldier's thinking. 'Behind that cliff lies the Valley of the Tombs of the Kings. We archaeologists have been excavating there on and off since 1819. It was an Italian, Belzoni, who first opened and wrote a description of the tomb of Pharaoh Seti I.'

Adamson looked at the Englishman in some amazement, but said nothing. The two men fell silent.

After an interval of several minutes Carter put a question. 'Do you know anything about the Nile?'

Remembering the incident of the previous evening, for which he was now more than thankful, the military policeman answered cautiously, 'A little, sir.'

'Well, it's the life-source of Egypt. We tend to forget that it's the second longest river in the world. It springs from the lakes in the African Highlands. Herodotus wrote "Egypt is the gift of the Nile" and he was correct.

'Just over a hundred and fifty miles up the river from here we find the first cataracts at Aswan. It is also the site of the great quarries from where the Pharaohs obtained their monolithic slabs of pink granite, from which they carved their statues. It was also at Aswan that the Ancient Egyptians, and indeed the Romans, measured the volume of water passing in the annual flood. In fact, we still use the Nilometre to this day. Gradations were carved in the smooth rock of Al Gezira, now called Elephant Island. It was one of the earliest places inhabited by man on the banks of the Nile.'

Adamson merely nodded, lost within his own thoughts, and still pondering his personal predicament. He betrayed little interest and Carter decided to say no more.

Ten minutes later they reached the quay above which, with some surprise, Adamson saw a somewhat battered old Ford. Carter strode up the steps of the bank and stepped into the vehicle. It was the last thing Adamson had expected and was apparently used to transport tourists. A couple of boxes were lifted from the ferry and placed in the boot. Without any instruction the driver started up the engine, climbed in and set off up the dusty track.

On each side the vegetation was lush. Small irrigation canals intersected the ground, creating tiny, irregular fields. Every now and then they saw the fellahin working the shaduf, the goat skins bulging with water from the primitive cisterns. Camels, donkeys and the occasional pony could be seen in the mud hut villages; chickens scattered in confusion at the noisy progress they made, while children rushed forward to observe with wide-eyed curiosity the mechanical monster.

Suddenly, in little over a mile, the terrain abruptly changed; the foliage gave way to sun-bleached rock and not a tree or shrub could be seen. The change of scenery assaulted the eyes;

hard, white and unremitting. Dust rose in billowing clouds and
they dare not move forward at more than a few miles per hour
for fear of the boulders strewn in their way. Minute by minute
the heat increased, radiating from the steep cliffs rising in the
distance with not a breath of wind.

Adamson had never before seen such desolation. He hoped
the equipment was ready to move. Carter stirred beside him
and pointed to a single-storey building on a rise of ground on
the right-hand side.

'That's where I live,' he said shortly.

Adamson was amazed. Not a bush, not a tree, nor any living
thing, until suddenly he looked to the sky. A solitary kite
wheeled in silent expectation. Carter again broke the silence.

'There are two main areas here: the Valley of the Queens and
the Valley of the Kings. In 1908 I was lucky enough to discover the mortuary temple of Queen Hatshepsût. It's over there,
on the left,' he pointed to the distance. 'We found two obelisks,
nearly one hundred feet tall, which we estimated must weigh
something in the region of three hundred and fifty tons each.
They had come down-river from Aswan. The queen dedicated
them to the god, Amun, and wrote "They who will behold my
mighty monuments in years to come will stand in awe at what
I have accomplished . . ." I also have a necklace that she wore,'
the archaeologist said casually.*

Still Adamson made no reply. This place did not appeal to
him.

They stopped for a few minutes to allow the engine to cool.
Carter discovered some coffee in an earthenware flask, provided
in a foodbox by the Winter Palace Hotel. Twenty minutes later
they continued over ever-rising ground with the cliffs, honey-
combed with small caves, beginning to press in upon them.
During this journey the army sergeant's reactions were suffering
a severe volte-face. If this was where Lord Carnarvon worked,
then he would far prefer to face the risks of the capital!

---

* Now in the temporary safe custody of Adamson. (1972.)

The car suddenly began to face a steeper incline and, as it did so, Carter said: 'Of course, there is not much social life around here.'

Which, in this barren desolation, was just about the most majestic understatement that Adamson had ever heard or was ever likely to hear.

Even before he could make reply, Carter continued: 'Anyway, I'm sure that won't worry you; we'll be cleared from the site in a week.'

To the Yorkshireman this statement came like a bombshell. Indeed, he doubted the veracity of his ears. He turned to look at the archaeologist, nestling comfortably in the corner of his seat.

'You mean, sir . . .' he began hesitatingly, '. . . that I'll have to come over here each day . . .'

In his heart he knew that this was not what Carter meant.

'Oh no,' was the casual reply. 'I'd prefer you to stay on site.'

With the ire beginning to bubble inside him Adamson yet kept a grip on his tongue. 'That's what you bloomin' well think,' he allowed himself the natural reaction.

At this precise moment the driver took a sharp, right-hand turn and there before them lay the legendary Valley of the Tombs of the Kings. They lurched and slithered down the loose stones and, within a few yards, came to rest near a collection of tents. The military policeman sat for a moment, still stunned, taking in the scene.

The cliff faces now towered above him, baking in the sunlight and shimmering heat. Kites wheeled on the strong up-currents against an azure sky and the only other sign of life were six Egyptian workmen toiling to remove a thirty-foot pile of sand and rubble rock chipping. But the overriding impression was one of stillness.

One of the workmen detached himself from the group and began to walk towards the car. Carter climbed out and went to meet him. They exchanged perfunctory greetings and the archaeologist surveyed the scene. Adamson alighted and stood

belligerently beside the prehistoric monster that gurgled and
steamed under the strain it had been asked to endure. He was
still not beaten and was determined to stand securely alongside
his only means of escape. After all, he was not a police sergeant
for nothing. What right had this man to dictate where he should
remain for the next seven days. He decided that by hook or by
crook he would somehow get back to Luxor.

'Now, sir, where is this equipment I'm supposed to collect?'
Adamson began, drawing himself up to his full height.

Carter seemed quite unconcerned.

'Over here, in the marquee,' he said, and led the way.

There were two army bell tents, khaki and drab, with a much
larger marquee, sandy-coloured, having been bleached by the
sun. The door flaps were rolled back.

'It will get hotter by this afternoon,' Carter murmured, as he
ducked within.

'There are your four boxes over there; you'll find the contents
in order with an inventory inside.'

'How are we supposed to get them down to the boat?' Adamson inquired, for they were large in size and obviously heavy.
Without waiting for a reply he continued: 'You're not sug-
gesting we take them down in that old jalopy, are you, sir?'

'Of course, but you will only be able to manage two at a
time.'

Adamson saw his chance.

'Very well, sir, I'll take two down this afternoon.'

Carter turned round: 'Look here,' he said softly. 'What do
I call you? Sergeant, Adamson, which would you like?'

Taken out of his stride the Yorkshireman said: 'Well, sir, my
first name is Richard. I'm not fussed either way.'

'Very well, Richard, now can't you understand that I'll need
you up here to look after this equipment before it's all sent
away. You won't be going to Luxor this afternoon; you are to
remain up here. I shall have all you require sent up from the
hotel.'

Adamson was too much the soldier not to know when he was

Tea on the terrace of the Grand Hotel, Luxor, 20 February 1904.

beaten. He had no recourse to higher authority, so he would
have to make the best of it. Slowly he began to take a keener
interest in his surroundings. There were two stretcher-like beds
in the marquee with rush mats on the floor, piles of boxes and
a trestle table.

'What about something to eat?' the surprising Carter inquired.

'Have we got anything, sir?'

'Of course, there is a box in the back of the car.'

They were interrupted by the head workman or 'boss
gaffir', as he was called, who asked Carter if he would like
any tea.

'No thank you,' was the rejoinder. 'We brought our food
with us.'

At which moment the driver of the car entered the marquee
carrying a large, square case containing their packed luncheon.
Carter immediately opened it, took out grapes, some melons and
a handful of oranges. Next came sandwiches, goats' milk in tall
stone jars and lemon juice.

Long before the discovery Howard out surveying on his Arab horse Sultan.

'Help yourself,' he invited, and sat down in one of the chairs. Placing his cap to one side, Adamson took a handful of sandwiches and began to eat.

'After luncheon I'll take you round the site and show you what we have been doing.'

There was an uncomfortable pause.

'Have you worked in this valley for long, sir?'

'On and off for twenty years,' was the matter-of-fact reply. Adamson was stunned.

Twenty minutes later they walked out into the full, stultifying heat of early afternoon.

'Would you like to see inside one of the tombs?' Carter asked his unwilling guest.

'Very well, sir,' was the begrudging reply.

The archaeologist called over one of the Egyptians who doubled as gatekeeper, and took a set of keys off him. He walked the few paces to the tomb of Rameses VI, inserted a massive key

and pulled open the heavy door. Handing a second torch to
Adamson, he led the way down a long, straight passage into the
bowels of the earth. As he did so, he flashed the torchbeam along
the walls, revealing magnificently, gaily painted frescoes, interlaced with ancient Egyptian inscriptions. The air was heavy, if
cool, and only their footsteps echoed in the emptiness. The
passage stretched ever downwards, wide enough to drive a car.
Hundreds of feet below they reached the main chambers, chipped
by hand from the living rock, meticulously square and sym-
metrical. The two men stood in silence, the one marvelling, in
spite of his familiarity with the scene; the other faintly interested, but very loath to show it.

Carter was now in a world of his own and was quite oblivious
of such human failings.

'This is where Rameses lay,' he murmured. 'In order to . . .
"go with quiet step towards the Other World." You see, Richard,
he expected to sleep here for three thousand years and, during
that time, the personality of the dead pharaoh was thought to
consist of four elements.' He pointed to the walls. 'There you
see the Khet representing the dead body; Shut the Shadow and
two of the unseen senses, the Ba and the Ka. The Ba took the
form of a human-headed bird which could fly round the subterranean passages of the tomb and thence out into the upper
air. It could refresh itself with water provided in a little trough
by the Sycamore Goddess. The Royal Ka, or spirit, had been
fashioned by Khnum on his wheel at the same time as he had
modelled the newborn child.

'The dead king would have to face his eternal judgement as
described in the Book of the Dead. He would be ushered into
the Hall of the Two Truths, saluting the Great God and his
forty-two assistants. He would declare that, although not entirely
perfect, he had shunned iniquity. Then he would begin to recite
thirty-six traditional negative statements; for instance: "I have
not acted sinfully towards men," "I have not obstructed the god
in his comings forth." Next he would go on to make his positive
statements: "I have satisfied the god with that which he

desires," "I have given bread to the hungry, water to the thirsty, clothing to the naked and a ferry to him who had no boat."

'Next he would plead, "Heart of my mother, heart of my various forms, rise not up against me as a witness. Oppose me not in the court of justice. Send not the balance down against me before the Guardian of the Scales. For thou art the Ka which is in my body, thou art Khnum who strengtheneth my limbs. Mayest thou attain to that Good whereto I aspire. Let not my name be in bad odour with the court. Speak no lie against me."

'His heart would then remain silent. The god, Anubis, would steady the scales and then joyfully declare that the two sides of his character balanced to perfection. Thoth would look upon the scales and happily confirm the dead pharaoh to be maa-kheru, or "true of voice".'

Carter suddenly stopped speaking, allowing his torchbeam to float over the walls of text and pictures which he had described, as if he were an arch priest of the other world. Suddenly, without a word, as if reluctant to break the spell, he began to retrace his steps back up the passage. Adamson meekly followed, somewhat chastened and silent. They shut the heavy gate behind them, walked a few yards and then Carter turned once more to look at the entrance.

To Adamson it all seemed so impossible to imagine. Outside, in the light of day, the mystery and magic of the tomb was almost scorched into unreality.

'You must understand, Richard, that the besetting fear of the pharaohs was that their sleep might be disturbed. It was for this reason that they chose such a remote and desolate valley, a mere crack in the earth, safe in its isolation, quiet in its solitude. You must agree they chose well.'

Adamson at least concurred with this.

'After the pharaoh had been laid to rest his tomb would be filled with those treasures and necessities required for his after-life. These articles would extend from items of the highest luxury down to his mummified food and wine. Upwards of a

The flight of steps that lead up to the Winter Palace Hotel from the banks of the Nile.

hundred and fifty slaves would be employed on the tomb, being kept in isolation for years.

'It was the tomb robber whom the priests and the pharaoh most feared. These jackals of their society were drawn like a magnet by their lust for gold, and constituted the main enemy. It was against them that the magical rites and incantations were performed. Then the walls of the individual chambers would be sealed and gradually, working their way back, the passages would be filled with the rock out-take from the original excavation. At last, when the royal seal had been imprinted in the mortar on the very last door, and when the final ceremony had been conducted by the high priest and his retinue, the slaves would be put to death. There is an inscription on Ineni's tomb which reads: "I, and I alone, supervised the building of a tomb for his majesty. No one else knew where it was, or ever heard about it." '

The Mortuary Temple of Queen Hatshepsût, now being restored. Note the towering cliff face and regal setting.

His story told, Carter handed his torch to Adamson. He turned and looked towards the group of workers. His driver squatted on the ground beside them, chatting. 'Mohammed,' he shouted. Carter walked towards the car. 'I shall go straight down to Luxor to collect your things. I'll send food over this evening. The rest will follow tomorrow. I'll see you in the morning.'

Adamson managed a fairly tight-lipped 'Very well, sir,' and began to walk towards the marquee. The driver came towards him, picked up the food hamper and six empty bottles, loaded them into the motor car, and started the engine. After making the necessary adjustment to the throttle he let in the clutch and the car jerked forward. Negotiating a wide circle they disappeared in a cloud of dust up the short, steep slope, and out of the entrance to the valley.

Richard Adamson walked back into the marquee, noticed a copy of the *Egyptian Gazette*, the English language newspaper which he had brought with him from Luxor, and sat down to read. He flicked idly through the pages and, as the sound of the motor car died away, he gradually became aware of the silence. The only sound in the cathedral-like atmosphere was the metallic clatter of metal shovels on stone. A few minutes later he walked outside and looked anew upon the scene. As he was doing so a young Egyptian labourer in his early twenties walked across with a steaming mug of coffee. His face was wreathed in welcoming smiles. 'My name, Abd-el-Maaboud,' was all he could say, but there was no doubting the warmth of his intentions.

'Sugar?' he gesticulated.

'No thanks, Abdul,' the army sergeant responded, with a soldier's typical mispronunciation. Adamson stood outside the tent sipping his drink.

The six workers laid down their tools and disappeared into their own tent. Great black shadows began to creep over the valley and utter silence reigned. Dusk swept in and the military policeman noticed the glow of an oil lamp through the canvas of the labourers' tent. Surely the car would return before darkness had fallen?

He decided to walk out of the valley and along the track to meet it. The rocks still radiated heat, absorbed from the sun of the day. It seemed to suffocate and smother his breathing. Adamson mentally remembered to watch out for cobras. Ten minutes later he saw the car, half a mile away. As he stood watching its progress a bat brushed in front of his face. He didn't like this place. Little did he know that it would become his home for seven long years. If he had known that, he would have started walking back to Cairo.

CHAPTER THREE

THE MUMMY'S HAND

IT would be difficult indeed to establish a common link between
Ireland and Egypt, if not impossible. But, if one thread might be
claimed, it would be an ability to commune with the spirits.
However, even the most trenchant, diehard folklore expert
would hardly expect the ghost of a long-dead Egyptian princess
to materialise in the borderlands of Tipperary.

Nevertheless, while Howard Carter was spending the evening
in Luxor and Adamson his first night in the Valley of the
Kings, the same waxing moon was also flooding with light the
evergreen fields of Ireland. It just so happened that in that
country a world-famous clairvoyant had made his temporary
home during the dark days of the 1914–18 war. He was of
Norman extraction, by name Louis Hamon, and thirty years
previously had also worked in the Valley of the Kings.

In the early eighteen nineties an undistinguished German
archaeologist, by name von Heller, had been excavating in the
Upper Nile area at Luxor, and had been profitably disposing of
mummies to museums and private collectors in Western Europe.
He was visited by and, indeed, shared the same roof as young
Louis Hamon. Hamon was widely travelled and had already
visited both China and India where he had studied mysticism
and the occult.

Fascinated by the history of the Ancient Egyptians he had
decided that, on his way home from the East, he would travel
up the Nile to visit the temples. At Karnak, that most awe-
inspiring of all Egyptian monuments, he had met and struck up

a friendship with von Heller, who was presently exploring the network of tombs in the Valley of the Kings.

He recounts that one evening they became lost underground, through lack of candles, and were forced to abandon any attempt to escape. On this occasion they had not taken with them the man they regarded as their chief guide, due to the fact that he was feeling unwell. Hamon decided that he would endeavour to contact this man through transference of thought. Whether or not he succeeded it would be difficult to tell, but certain it was that this Egyptian eventually found them. From that moment the two men established a strong rapport.

Late on the night prior to his departure for England Hamon received a visitor, his friend, their principal guide. He beckoned him to follow into the depths of the Temple of Karnak, beside which they were encamped. When they reached the Hall of Columns he was told to wait and, a few minutes later, the man reappeared. He was carrying an object wrapped in cloth. Bending down and, without saying a word, he proceeded to unwrap it. To the somewhat startled surprise of Hamon the Egyptian produced the right hand of a mummy, apparently in an excellent state of preservation. It was delicate, obviously that of a woman, the finger nails perfect in shape, covered with gold leaf. On the first finger a gold ring shone, upon which he could see minute hieroglyphics. The hand itself appeared solid, nut-brown, as if carved from a solid block of wood. The bones, where it had been severed at the wrist, were white and gleaming. The Egyptian then recounted this story which he said had been handed down to him by his father, from his father, and for generations.

He claimed that his ancestors were descended from the priests of Karnak. The hand was reputed to have originally belonged to the Princess Makitaten, seventh daughter of the Pharaoh Akhenaten, the heretic king. Akhenaten, whose first wife was Nefertiti, remains the most fascinating, humanistic and intellectually brilliant of all the pharaohs throughout the dynasties. He, it was, who broke the power of priesthood, removed the royal court from Thebes,* and established himself at Tel-el-Amarna. When, after many years on the throne, Akhenaten finally died, this particular daughter raised an army and marched against Thebes. She was not successful, the Thebans winning the day.

The princess was killed and the priests, wishing to make maximum capital from their victory, hacked off her hand, duly embalmed it, and placed it in the Temple of Karnak for all to witness as a reminder not to usurp the power of the priesthood. 'Within this hand is the Ka of Princess Makitaten and I hand it to you for safe keeping. One day, many years hence, the Ka will wish to make its escape and return to the mummified body lying beside the tomb of her father. Until that time I commit it to your care.'

Louis Hamon returned to England, where he quickly established himself as an exceptional seer and clairvoyant, and used the hand of the princess as his talisman. It never left his side. His father did not like his use of the family name and, therefore, Count Louis Hamon adopted the pseudonym, Cheiro, which word he made famous throughout the world. He derived it from the Greek root, Cheir, meaning the hand, and it was pronounced Ki-ro.

It was before the First World War and thereafter, when spiritualism and clairvoyance reached its peak, that he enjoyed his greatest success. Previously he had predicted the exact date of Queen Victoria's death, and the year and month when Edward VII would pass away. He foretold the destiny of the Tsar of Russia, the assassination of King Humbert of Italy, and the attempt on the Shah's life while he had been staying in Paris. He read the hands of Sarah Bernhardt, Mark Twain, Joseph Chamberlain, Sir Austen Chamberlain, Sir Arthur Sullivan, Nellie Melba and a host of others. Not least among his clients was Lord Carnarvon, who was intensely interested in the occult and spiritualism.

* Now Luxor.

Now, in 1922, with Ireland racked by political strife, Count Louis and his wife decided to return to England.

Throughout the previous thirty years the hand had been kept on a purple velvet cushion and was always on display in Cheiro's salon. They were now packing up their furniture and chattels when he suddenly discovered, for the first time, that the hand was beginning to alter in substance and appearance. Whereas, previously, it had been as rigid as a polished piece of ebony, now it appeared that the flesh was tending to become soft and pliable. To his utter astonishment, a day or two later, he noticed what appeared to be minute globules of blood glistening on the knuckles and larger spots of blood oozing from the fingertips.

Hamon was the proprietor of a local factory in which he had been converting peat into activated carbon for use as a filter in gas masks, but, by the end of the war, business was dropping away. He employed an English chemist who had worked with him since 1920.

Puzzled and anxious about the mummy's hand he asked his chemist to examine it. His employee took it to his laboratory to analyse the blood under a microscope. Within a few hours he reported that there was little doubt that the blood was human. So far as the decomposition of the hand was concerned he could only suggest that perhaps the limb could be restored to its former rigidity by immersing it in a solution of pitch and shellac. Hamon agreed he should try and this treatment did stop the bleeding, but not for very long.

In fact, it was on 31 October, when the contents of his house had been packed, that Count Hamon and his wife were forced to decide what to do about the hand. One thing now seemed certain; in its present condition of accelerating decay they could not take it with them. Indeed, it now lay on its velvet cushion, the last remaining article in the salon, awaiting disposal. During the latter part of the evening they suddenly decided that possibly cremation would be the apposite solution. Hamon decided to build up the fire in his hall in order to provide sufficient heat for the task in hand. In order to give it time to build up he and his wife decided to take a stroll in the garden.

The night was clear and the moon four days short of full. When they returned they noticed that their Irish staff had laid dinner on the table in the dining-room and had opened all the windows of the room. This repast had not, of course, been prepared for their master and mistress, but was a quaint Irish custom that bade welcome to the spirits of those departed. Until this moment the significance of the date had escaped them. It was, of course, Hallowe'en.

Without more ado Cheiro fetched the ebony stand bearing the mummy's hand and took it through to the hall. His wife, who had long been interested in Egyptology and who had visited the country, suddenly suggested that they should say a prayer.

Familiar with the Book of the Dead, she recited some verses:

> Thy flesh have I given unto thee,
> Thy bones have I kept for thee,
> Thy members have I collected,
> Thou art set in order;
> Thou seest the Gods,
> Thou settest out on thy way,
> Thine hand reaches beyond the horizon and unto
> The holy place where thou wouldst be.

Leaning forward, Cheiro thrust the mummified hand deep into the glowing fire, stand, cushion and all, including the gold ring on the finger. Immediately flames of great brilliancy shot up around it and there was a distinct aroma of spices in the air. They watched for quite some time until all was consumed. Then, their task completed, they decided to retire to bed.

It was a clear, calm night, but at the very moment they had turned to mount the stairs, their backs toward the entrance hall, a sudden rushing of wind brought them to a premature halt. They both instinctively turned round, for even in a matter of split parts of a second, the wind seemed to be gathering tremendous force and began to batter at the heavy oak doors.

The couple were frankly terrified and stood rooted to the ground. A great pressure seemed to be building up against the doors until, with a crash, they burst wide open. But there was nothing to be seen; only the moonlit garden.

The atmosphere became singularly cold. Suddenly, beyond the portal, something caught their attention and began to materialise. With an undefinable shape it started to move through the porch and into the hall, where gradually its outline and figure began to develop into that of a woman. However, the form stopped short at the hips. It was very beautiful; a remarkable face that finally looked towards them. Nobility, grandeur and pride of race seemed marked in every line.

She wore what appeared to be a headdress, formed by the wings of beetles, fashioned in beaten gold, the ends of which rested gracefully on her shoulders. In the centre of her forehead was a golden asp, the emblem of Egyptian royalty.

The figure moved deeper into the hall and gazed at Hamon and his wife. Both her hands were clasped together, as if in a moment of ecstasy. She appeared to be trying to speak and her lips began to move, but no sound emanated. Suddenly she threw back her head, lifted her hands slowly in the form of an arch, and bowed towards them. Then, as briefly she had come, she began to drift away, still remaining in the same posture, but retreating backwards through the door until she was lost in the night.

The experience was so frightening that Count Hamon and his wife dared not go to bed. It was not until the cold light of dawn that reality and their courage began to return. It was not to be the last visitation of the spirit.

Hamon decided to rake out the cold ashes of the fire and in them he found the individual bones of the hand, white and calcined. He decided to collect them, thinking that one day he might return them from whence they had come some thirty years earlier. Also in the deep white ash he found the gold ring, unaffected by the heat of the fire.

When Sergeant Richard Adamson awoke in the Valley of the Kings the sun was already shining. He quickly got up and shaved in cold water. He ate the fruit and the last of the sandwiches for breakfast. The Egyptians were also astir and brought him a mug of hot coffee. However, they did not attempt to set about their work, explaining that they would wait the arrival of Mr Howard Carter. At 8.30 the archaeologist appeared. With a casual 'Good morning, Richard,' he inquired if Adamson had enjoyed a restful night.

Carter walked down to where the labour force had slowly foregathered and spent some minutes with them. Apparently, in their previous excavations, Carter had stopped short of the north-east corner of Rameses' tomb. Now they were trenching southwards through the mound and also through a number of ancient huts, probably constructed by the original excavators three thousand years before.

Having given his instructions Carter walked back to the marquee.

'Did they deliver everything you needed from Luxor last night?'

'Yes, thank you, sir.'

Adamson tried his very last throw.

'Shall I be going back to Luxor this evening, Mr Carter?' he queried in some temerity. Carter looked at him sharply, but paused for a moment or two, as if to contain his impatience.

'Look, I thought I explained to you that we will be finished here in ten days' time. Yesterday was the first of the ten days; today it leaves nine. I require you to stay here until the task is completed. Then you can leave with the stores.'

Adamson knew when he was beaten. The man was not to be drawn. He suddenly decided, not before time, that it would be politic not to mention the subject again. Somewhat to his surprise Carter suddenly divested himself of his overcoat and, grasping a shovel, went out to join the workmen.

The sergeant looked upon the scene with cumulated aversion. If he was being forced to stay in this god-forsaken spot, certainly it was not incumbent upon him to dig! He pointedly walked away from the scene of activity, along the path to the entrances of several other tombs. The hours of the morning dragged on slowly but remorselessly.

Just over four hours later, at 1 p.m., utterly bored and seeing no sign of a break in the work, Adamson walked down and accosted Carter.

'Are you going to have something to eat, sir?'

The man looked up, as if mentally remote. The sergeant could not but feel a sense of grudging admiration. No wonder he had detected in the Arab labourers a deep sense of respect for the man for whom they were working.

'Oh yes, I think that'll do for me today. I have to go down to Luxor this afternoon.'

In spite of his good intentions of a few hours before Adamson could not hold his tongue.

'Shall I come with you, sir?' he asked in unbridled enthusiasm.

'No, I shall send more supplies for you this evening. Is there anything special you would like?'

'Yes, sir, I'll make out a list,' the policeman declared belligerently. With that Adamson stalked off towards the marquee, with an unruffled Carter walking in behind him. He quickly searched for a piece of paper, grasped a pencil, and made his first requests.

It says something for the archaeologist that, having read the list through, he made no comment; simply folded the paper and placed it in his pocket. Adamson then sat down and attacked the sandwiches.

Day followed day and gradually the mound of rubble diminished, while Lord Carnarvon arrived back in England.

The fifth earl, christened George Edward Stanhope Molyneux

Herbert, Lord Porchester, was aged fifty-four and was known by his family and intimates as 'Porchy'. He was a remarkable man. Of a frail disposition as a child, at nine he suffered the bitter blow of losing his mother in childbirth. However, blessed and comforted by being a member of a large family in a privileged and protected society, he managed, within these confines, to enjoy tremendous freedom. Unfortunate in the choice of his preparatory school, he nevertheless liked Eton and finally went up to Trinity College, Cambridge.

Even at that stage he was nurturing a passion for 'collecting'. He began in those tiny shops and curio houses that press shoulder to shoulder in the little streets and alleys of the university town. Originally intended for a military career his physical health, if not his spirit, precluded such a vocation. Having learned to sail when holidaying at his father's villa at Porto Fino the urge to travel came upon him with a passion and, by the age of twenty-one, aboard the yacht *Aphrodite*, he had embarked upon a world-wide voyage.

With a great sense of fun and a positive tease he was eventually able to mix in all stratum of life, often enjoying more fully the company of simple, if unusual, characters with whom he found a special affinity.

He was dreadfully untidy and lax about the minutiae of everyday life. To receive a letter from him would be something of a miracle and his wardrobe was only conspicuous by the fact that it never changed. Of a benign personality, he was a friend to everybody, but if rare occasion demanded he was perfectly capable of either asserting his authority or registering a contrary point of view. He delighted in the quirks of human character. It was perhaps tragic that such an amiable man was to his eldest son almost a father unknown. This was, without doubt, due to the then traditional style of an aristocratic family's upbringing, rather than any lack of affection. In those days children were certainly not seen and, if possible, definitely not heard.

Succeeding to his father's title at the age of twenty-three, he married at twenty-nine and was persuaded, no doubt to the general relief of his family, to invest in a new frock coat. However, upon hasty return to Highclere Castle he immediately changed to his old suit of tweeds.

He loved motor car driving and was always accompanied by his trusted chauffeur who had been in his employ for twenty-eight years. He studied photography and became noted for a unique ability and artistry which saw recognition when he was elected President of the Camera Club of Great Britain. He was a connoisseur of art to such effect that dealers would seek his unbiased arbitration. He loved horses and built the now famous Highclere Stud, the progeny of which have contested the 'Classics' from then to the present day.

It was a cause of considerable regret to him that, due to his frailty of health, he was unable to take an active part in the war.

Lord Carnarvon had been worried to the point of distraction for the safety of his eldest son, Lord Porchester, who had fought through the Mesopotamia campaign and was now stationed in India. Before leaving, in 1916, his heir had asked him to take special care of Susie, his little fox terrier bitch. Lord Carnarvon had happily agreed and was distraught when, upon a visit to London, the dog was run over by a taxi and its life only saved by the amputation of one of its forelegs. Fortunately it found this handicap no great burden, other than accumulating a little extra fat, and enjoyed its life and sleeping in a basket at the foot of his lordship's bed.

Lord Carnarvon also became interested in spiritualism and the study of the occult. Many séances were held at Highclere Castle, the vogue growing in the years following the pitiful loss of life in the war.

It had been a great disappointment to Carnarvon when, a few months previously, he and Howard Carter had agreed that it was pointless taking out another concession in the valley, for now they had covered every square metre of ground. His sadness was occasioned, not so much by the fact that his huge

financial investment in the project had come to no avail, but
more so because his close friend and partner had not succeeded
in the task that had become his life's aim. It had proven an
equal disappointment to his daughter, Lady Evelyn Herbert,
for she had accompanied her father on many of his visits to
Egypt.

Since the end of the war she had become his inseparable companion, the relationship happily progressing from the era of
'to be seen and not heard' to that in which they sought each
other's company, enjoying a love and respect for each other
which was to enrich their lives.

Evelyn was just twenty-one years of age.

Work in the valley continued. The large mound of rubble
gradually began to disappear and they demolished another series
of ancient huts that had been built in front of the Ramesside
tomb. During this work, which was still well above bedrock
level, Carter only visited the site at 10 a.m. and again at 4 p.m.
He had explained to Adamson that he was packing the
contents of his house. Apparently, he had acquired his
furniture from Luxor and was making arrangements for its
return.

For his part Adamson had begun to assume a greater interest
in the dig, following Carter's description of his tireless en-
deavours and his amazing belief that he would eventually find
his tomb. The military policeman could not resist making a
pointed rejoinder: 'Aren't you leaving it a little bit late,
sir?'

Carter merely smiled.

'I've been working here on and off for twenty-odd years and
I wouldn't have done so unless I had some substantial facts to
work on.'

'And what are they, sir, may I ask?'

'We have three major pieces of evidence. A faience cup found
beneath a rock; the gold foil from a small pit tomb, bearing the
figures and name of Tutankhamen and his queen; and finally,

some material which we believe was used during the funeral ceremonies of the king.'

He further explained, to the somewhat incredulous soldier, that until the very last foot of ground had been turned he would still have faith.

'If there is anything to be found this is where we will find it,' had been his final statement. He had then shown Adamson his working map, drawn in the form of a grid, upon which every square metre of ground had been recorded as it had been cleared to bedrock level. Even Adamson was reduced to silent admiration, recognising the extent of the mammoth operation this man had undertaken.

Thousands of miles away in Ireland a strange event had occurred the previous afternoon. The impassioned 'Troubles' had reached such a high pitch of intensity that rumour had it that the Republican rebels were about to attack the main military barracks in Dublin. Count Louis Hamon and his wife had been warned the previous day, by members of the rebel army, that they were going to destroy the railway bridges along the track running to Dublin. Accordingly, the English couple had expedited their departure and had boarded the last express bound for Dublin. The train was packed with regular soldiers and they could only find two seats in the Pullman immediately behind the engine. Two troopers helped them lift their cases on to the racks above their heads. The train gathered speed amidst intermittent choruses of ribald songs.

Something over an hour later the train was fast approaching its destination, with the coaches rocking rhythmically on the rails. Cheiro, who had been dozing, awoke and happened to look up at the cases above his wife's head. A strange fluttering movement had attracted his eye; with a start he realised that the label on one particular valise was spinning and twisting in agitated contortions, whereas all the other labels along the rack were swaying gently in time with the wheels. Even as his mind was becoming fully alert Cheiro recalled in the instant that in this particular case was the bottle in which he had placed the bones of the mummy's hand. Even before he had had a chance to consider the situation rationally he had an overwhelming feeling that he should take down the cases immediately.

Hardly had he obeyed the impulse, to the not inconsiderable irritation of his travelling companions, than the train began to lurch violently as emergency braking was applied. In a second all was confusion. The remaining luggage on the racks spewed on to the floor, soldiers were pitched across the carriage, until suddenly the train jerked to a premature halt just within a station.

In seconds they realised that all the buildings were on fire and that burning timbers were beginning to fall on the engine. The nameboards announced that it was Liffey Junction.

Although they were unaware of it, yet another danger was at hand. Apparently the rebels had uncoupled the express of the Galway Mail standing in the terminus at Dublin. They had opened wide its throttle to send it thundering down the track towards the oncoming express and the army reinforcements. By a miracle it was switched, moments before head-on collision.

Count Louis Hamon and his wife sped across Dublin and

Castle Carter' as Howard Carter's bungalow was affectionately known. It still stands, a cool building, amidst sun-scorched rock and sand with temperatures frequently above 100°. It was Carter's haven of peace amidst the barren desolation.

caught the boat for England. Safely aboard the vessel they began to discuss the frightening experience and Cheiro told his **wife** of his intuition; or had it been a warning? Was it preposterous to believe that the spirit of the dead princess had endeavoured to save them?

CHAPTER FOUR

SEAL OF THE NECROPOLIS

IT was during the afternoon of 3 November 1922, that Richard
Adamson decided to take a stroll to the disused huts atop the
Rameses' tomb and take a few photographs. It had been a hot
and beautiful day, with the kites soaring far above his head. All
was still and peaceful. He completed his task and began to
retrace his steps along the steep, down-curving path, twenty or
thirty feet above the heads of the four Egyptian labourers. As
he was carefully picking his way over the crushed chippings he
heard a shout, which was so unusual as to cause him to halt in
his tracks and peer down. There was a distinct buzz of excitement between the four workers who were standing in a rect-
angular hole of some ten or twelve feet that they had cleared
within the foundations of the huts.

At first glance Adamson could see that they had uncovered
what appeared to be eight or nine very large boulders. To his
untrained eye they seemed of little significance although, up
until this time, there had been only small-sized chippings to
remove. One of the men shouted to his other two companions
working some distance away. Adamson realised that they were
closely examining a piece of ground a foot or two from the
actual boulders.

There was little doubt that these experienced excavators knew
immediately that they had found something, but what? There
was a deal of agitated discussion and argument and, as he
approached, the boss gaffir smiled at Adamson and pointed to
the ground. The British military policeman stared curiously and

saw that a few inches beneath the surface yet another block of stone lay almost entirely buried. This one was of a distinctly different shape and, so far as he could see amidst the sand and rubble, it looked somewhat similar to a four-foot kerb stone. He decided to take one of two photographs and, having done so, noticed that the workers were watching him in a distinctly changed manner.

Suddenly the excitement seemed to subside. The fifth and sixth workmen, who had joined the group, pointedly walked back to their own piece of excavation. The others continued to talk somewhat sporadically and then, picking up their shovels, began to throw back a large quantity of chippings and sand. Shortly the boulders had disappeared again; then tools were downed for the night.

To Adamson there was nothing much untoward about the situation, although he had noted with but the barest feeling of curiosity that the normally happy acceptance of his presence had seemed for a few minutes to have changed to a sense of resentment. Anyway he could see no reason to be greatly excited over a few odd boulders and he dismissed the matter from his mind. Obviously they could not have had that much significance, otherwise they would not have re-covered them.

Deep shadows engulfed the valley; the kites returned to their ledges and silence reigned. As the vaulted heavens lit up with starlight, a magnificent moon, one night short of full, began to ride across the sky. Adamson lit his hurricane lamps and prepared his evening meal.

On the morning of 4 November the sun tipped the ridge of the cliffs as she had done for countless thousands of years. The ancients believed that the sky was an azure blue sea upon which the stars merely sailed and, noting that they and the sun disappeared in the west only to arise again in the east, concluded that they could only return by way of a subterranean river that must flow through the underworld from west to east. It was in this Kingdom of the Dead that the god, Osiris, and his wife, Isis, reigned supreme.

Richard Adamson awoke at the normal hour, washed and made his breakfast. He was in no untoward hurry; there was nothing to distinguish the day. However, although the Egyptian excavators eventually came out of their tents, having made their usual morning coffee, they seemed in no hurry to get down to work. Indeed they seemed hesitant to begin. As had happened on the previous two mornings Carter arrived somewhat late. When he did so, he walked down the path towards the marquee.

'Good morning, Richard,' he began and immediately noticed that the workers were not actually engaged in digging. His eyes suddenly fired with intuitive interest and shifted back to Adamson.

'What's happened?' he asked.

'Nothing, sir,' came the reply.

'Then why aren't they working?'

'I don't know, sir. They did find some boulders.'

'Boulders,' repeated Carter curiously, for up to now the area had given up only small flints and sand. 'Where were they?' he continued, looking down towards the site.

'Over there,' Adamson pointed. 'They've covered them up again.'

Carter's eyes shifted back again and the thought flashed through Adamson's mind, 'Yes, that's funny; I wonder what made them do that. Perhaps the blighters were anxious for Carter not to see them for they knew that the Concession was about to end.'

'Very well,' Carter said, without any undue interest, but true to his meticulous character. 'We'll uncover them again.'

'Right, sir,' Adamson replied smartly. By now, after his lecture of some days previously, he had begun to take a more positive interest in the excavation activity.

He walked down the slope, even before Carter. All four Egyptians looked up at him. 'We'll uncover the boulders again,' he gesticulated, and they smiled . . .

c

Carter and Adamson stood side by side as the shovels gradually disclosed the boulders. They looked completely nondescript, were in no precise position, but they were unexpected.

'The other slab of stone was just down beside those, sir. It's a bit lower beneath the surface.'

All was still, save the clink of shovels biting into the chip. Gradually they reached bedrock level until, there before them the oblong piece of stone came into view. Carter stiffened, his eyes now distinctly alert. Almost instinctively the Egyptians turned to look up at him. Within a second he was down alongside them and grasping a trowel; next he picked up a shovel to throw up the rubble. He now began to scratch the sand away from the edges, up out of the pit. Suddenly Adamson also found himself picking up a shovel for the very first time, in order to prevent the sand from falling back down the banks.

There seemed to be a feverish tension in the archaeologist's body. Within minutes he began to tackle the ground alongside the stone.

'It's something,' he began to mutter.

Gradually two of the Egyptians became caught up in the early tremors of excitement and moved in beside him, excavating the sand on either side and throwing it into their baskets.

'It . . . it could be a step,' Carter suddenly exclaimed, taking off his hat and throwing down his coat. As he started again he muttered, as if to himself: 'Perhaps it's a cache?'

The sound of metal now began to sing as it resounded off the solid stone. Could perhaps a sleeping pharaoh even now begin to hear the first minute sounds of intrusion? But, if indeed he was able to hear, no sense of fear would it cause him. For he would know that Anubis, the jackal-headed god, had simply arrived to welcome him at the end of his three-thousand-year journey, and carry his soul to the Judgement Hall.

'Be careful . . . be careful,' Carter kept saying, his voice becoming strident with pent-up emotion. 'Keep level, I say. My God, what have we found?'

As the shovels of the workmen revealed what appeared to be

a long, flat stone, Carter again took up the trowel. Deftly, without undue speed and exercising utmost caution, he began to excavate the very extremities of the stone. He said absolutely nothing, but his body was rigid with tension and his hands seemed to flick at the sand and chipping with nervous hypertension. Not a word was spoken by anyone; even the kites, wheeling hundreds of feet above, seemed to pause in their flight, eyes riveted on the little knot of men.

The trowel swept across the far top side of the stone and encountered living rock. Thrusting it deep into the nearside sand it again came into touch with something solid. Carter's hands froze. It was as if he hardly dare formulate the words. He paused for another breathless second, staring intently at the ground.

'It's a step,' he said simply. 'It's definitely a step.'

He looked up and caught the eyes of Adamson and then flashed round to his workmen. He looked back again; this time his communication was almost to himself.

'A vault . . . maybe . . . maybe only a cache . . .'

Within a few seconds the mask of his professional calm returned. He beckoned one of the men and indicated where he should commence with his shovel.

'Be careful,' he said yet again. 'Be careful. Not too fast, there may be something under here. Richard, don't let the rubble pile up; spread it back on the top; we may have to excavate in that direction very shortly.'

Indeed, within half an hour, it was no longer possible for Carter to continue himself. Two steps were clear, but above the third were at least two feet of chipping. He stepped aside and climbed out, indicating where the men should proceed. Suddenly he glanced up, as if studying anew the significance of the position and direction of the steps in relation to the entrance to the tomb of Rameses VI. It was, incredibly, only a mere thirteen feet from that tomb's entrance. Dare he hope that this could be the end of his twenty-year search.

Time stood still. Baskets of stone flashed out of the pit until all were perspiring. Sand kept trickling down from the edges and Adamson endeavoured to scrape it further back, as Carter had demanded.

Half an hour later the archaeologist stepped back into the pit and it was not long before he was able to demarcate the edges on all its three sides of what was obviously a stairway. The sun traversed the chasm, but never a moment did they pause throughout the day, such was their excitement. The other two workers had long since joined them and now all six were feverishly removing ever more rubble. Richard Adamson could now see Carter in another light. Here was the artistic temperament, highly strung, propelled by a limitless flow of nervous energy.

Three lines of thought were erupting in Carter's brain. Instinctively he began to think of his friend and patron, Lord Carnarvon. Oh, how he wished he were here. Whatever awaited them at the bottom, whether limited success or even bitter disappointment, this was the heart and stuff of archaeology. If only . . . if only it could be the tomb of Tutankhamen.

If it was, no wonder it had escaped detection, for the ground whereon they now worked had been covered by hundreds upon hundreds of tons of rubble excavated from the later tomb of Rameses VI. If it had escaped the detection of the tomb robbers during the first twenty or thirty years after its closure, there might yet be a chance that for once a royal tomb would be found undespoiled. Carter cursed himself for allowing such thoughts. He must not dream, but yet the chipped stairway, for such it appeared to be, began to turn his faculties feverish.

Suddenly both Egyptians and Englishmen realised that they were lost in shadow, the sun having traversed the valley. Without a word everyone stopped working, scrambled out and stood in silence, contemplating the scene. Carter's hand went to the shoulder of the boss gaffir. They looked at one another and the smile they exchanged was serene. Two professional excavators knew, in their hearts, that they were now descending and fighting their way to something, at least, of importance. Any reward, after having removed 200,000 tons of rubble, would be some consolation.

The group moved wearily towards the marquee. They were covered in dust, tired, thirsty and hungry. They soon made amends.

Suddenly Carter's eye lifted to the sky. He became conscious that the valley was now flooded with moonlight. There, hanging high above him, against a velvet backdrop sky, a totally full moon peered down at him, as if it were in sorrow. Adamson was just clearing away when Carter turned to him. 'Richard, I am afraid I'll have to ask you to sit out the night on the steps.'

The military policeman could not believe his ears.

'Do what, sir?' he inquired incredulously.

Carter looked at him sternly and did not move his eyes in the direction of their other companions.

'I shall want you to spend the night on the steps.'

There was no mistaking his meaning. So far they had uncovered ten steps and no one knew how many might remain. Adamson caught the look in Carter's eye.

'Very well, sir, just as you say.'

Quietly exhilarated Carter rode out down the valley. As he left it behind him the cliffs, illumined white by the moonbeams, slipped away and only the boulders and flat desolation remained.

Adamson collected two blankets and, somewhat reluctantly, took up his sentinel position. The Egyptians retired to their tents, their oil lamps just visible through the sun-bleached canvas. They chattered, as the Arabs will, their voices low, earnest, spiced with speculation. At least, they surmised, there would be more work.

Howard Carter rode down the slopes in exaltation. Suddenly the voice of a hyena bayed at the moon. The donkey pricked its ears and Carter wondered whether Anubis was out on the prowl.

The night was long. Howard Carter tossed and turned in feverish expectation, his high-ceilinged, ground-floor bedroom a treasure-house of thoughtful speculation. Richard Adamson also suffered the longest night of his life. Even a man without imagination might wonder who had trodden those rock steps before, but dawn came at last for everyone.

Coffee was brewed by the Egyptians; Adamson cast the sand from his clothing and Carter mounted his donkey. Within an hour they were all hard at work again. Gradually, as the steps descended, the western edge of the pit began to run underground. Shortly it was completely roofed in and the hole became a passage measuring some ten feet by six feet wide.

An hour or so later, amidst a surge of excitement, the excavators uncovered a large, wooden lintel, beneath which the plasterwork of a sealed door began to appear.

'Be careful, be careful,' Carter implored, as basket after basket of rubble was carried out up the stairs. Now the archaeologist could ill-conceal the excitement that motivated every action of his body as he dug and clawed at the rubble. Was this the tomb of a noble? Had plunderers been there before him? Dare he believe that it might be *the* royal tomb he had been seeking? Yet the smallness and comparative insignificance of the approach compared ill-favourably with the other royal tombs in the valley.

It was with a thrill bordering on euphoria that Carter stabbed his finger at the well-known seal of the Necropolis, depicting the Jackal and nine captives. But, as yet, there was no cartouche of a king. Step by step, basket by basket, they descended, all the while revealing lower portions of the door. Certain it was that the tomb had been constructed for a person of very high standing.

Carter could contain himself no longer. Seizing a trowel he began to excavate a small hole in the plaster just beneath the lintel. He made it only large enough to be able to insert an electric torch. This, as it transpired, was hardly necessary for, as he pressed his face to the plaster, he could see that behind was a passage filled, tight packed, with rubble. Without pausing for a moment they continued to dig on down toward the base of the door.

Work continued, hour upon hour, and Richard Adamson watched in fascination the archaeologist at work, peering intently at each and every seal imprinted in the plaster. As an ever greater expanse of the door became revealed, Carter's excitement became marginally subdued. 'Only the Necropolis seal . . .' he kept murmuring to himself; until, by four o'clock in the hot afternoon, they seemed to have reached the final step of the stairway. In all fourteen had now been exposed.

Carter stood back, like a man well satisfied, and then, to Adamson's surprise, began to fill in the peephole he had made beneath the lintel. Brushing over the entire surface of the door, he now examined it minutely. It was obviously in keeping with the style of the Eighteenth Dynasty. Could it be the tomb of a nobleman, or was it a royal cache? But now, at least, it looked somewhat unlikely that it could be the tomb of Tutankhamen, for nowhere was his personal seal revealed.

Carter turned and looked up the long flight of steps. He would now mount them as no one had done for well over three thousand years. Even that was a privilege, a moment to be savoured. He ascended in silent exaltation.

'Now then, Richard, our next task is to seal this stairway completely.'

The soldier, in khaki bush jacket and shorts, said never a word.

'I am not going to go any further. Lord Carnarvon must share our achievement. I shall cable him tomorrow.'

'Very good, sir,' Adamson answered and, with the merest twinkle in his eye, said lightly: 'I suppose this will put paid to Luxor completely!'

'Great heavens, yes.' Carter reacted, not comprehending the underlying humour. 'Yes, you'll have to stay here; there's no knowing what awaits us inside this tomb. We'll have, at least, a three-week delay before Lord Carnarvon can reach us.'

Adamson stood before his master in painful and abject silence.

'Come on, cheer up,' Carter laughed at his expression. 'Is there anything else you will need?'

'There certainly will be, Mr Carter. I'll go and make out another list.' With that he stomped into the marquee, snatched some paper and stabbed at it with the butt of a pencil.

List of items required by Sgt Adamson:

1. A decent gramophone.
2. Records: Musicals, light opera, operetta, especially Chu Chin Chow.
3. Uniform from my barracks in Cairo.
4. My medal ribbons.
5. Books: Edgar Wallace and crime.
6. Extra tropical kit.
7. Toilet requisites and confectionery.

'That'll do for a start,' he thought to himself. 'We'll see what he says to this little lot.'

Howard Carter scrutinised the list but again said nothing. To his credit, in due course, every request was fulfilled. The valley was never quite the same again, as the brooding silence of the night was shattered by many a West End musical, not to mention arias from *Traviata* and *Madame Butterfly*. It was enough to awaken any pharaoh from his sleep.

After urgent consultation with the gaffir it was decided to bridge over the open passage with planks. Having done so they stretched tarpaulins across and secured these with ropes and wooden tent pegs. Next they began to load it with rubble and boulders. Higher and higher the mound rose until, in a couple of hours, the site was transformed almost to its original appearance.

Once again darkness descended and the archaeologist addressed himself to the soldier. 'Tomorrow I shall go to Luxor to cable England and also inform the authorities in Cairo. Your job is now Security. I don't have to tell you how important it is. Good night, Richard; it's been a wonderful day.'

'Yes, sir,' the soldier agreed, with somewhat mixed feelings. He was now beginning to wonder if he would ever be relieved of his wretched isolation.

On the following morning, 6 November, Carter cabled his patron. Its receipt, at Highclere Castle, dropped like a bolt from the blue. It was delivered in the early morning. Unsuspectingly the fifth earl lifted the envelope from the silver salver. He slit it open and read the following:

AT LAST HAVE MADE WONDERFUL DISCOVERY IN VALLEY; A MAGNIFICENT TOMB WITH SEALS INTACT; RE-COVERED SAME FOR YOUR ARRIVAL; CONGRATULATIONS. HOWARD CARTER.

His lordship could hardly believe his eyes. He told his servant to find Lady Evelyn. His twenty-one-year-old daughter simply leapt with excitement, but her father's response was completely in character; he played it cool.

'Papa, how marvellous! Quick, we must find the times of boats to Alexandria.'

Mentally the normally self-assured young lady had already set sail.

'Come, come Evelyn, my darling, there's no need for haste. Don't be so theatrical.'

But his lordship's outward calm could not withstand the accumulating excitement of the day. As more and more people read the cable enthusiasm generated enthusiasm. By nightfall Carnarvon himself was poring over the lists of sailings during the next few days.

He knew he must reply to Carter and, with sublime understatement, cabled: 'POSSIBLE COME SOON.'

Howard Carter received this on the 8th, followed almost immediately by a second directive: 'PROPOSE ARRIVE ALEXANDRIA 20TH.'

Carter now sent a telegram to his friend and erstwhile assistant Callender, who had helped him on many previous excavations. That gentleman responded with alacrity and presented himself the following day.

Even in 1922 news of any discovery would sweep through the country, as it did on this occasion. It was two days later that Adamson heard the sound of a motor car. He was somewhat surprised, because Carter had told him that he would not be coming back to the valley for at least ten days, while he worked in Luxor to prepare for a major excavation.

In fact this carload of people was the prelude of thousands to come. Much to his amazement Adamson discovered that they were Americans, tourists on holiday at the Winter Palace Hotel. He had no authority to keep them away, but it was the boss gaffir who took charge of the incident. He was well used to dealing with the idle, the rich and the curious, and promptly sent them on their way. Adamson was lost in admiration.

Carter worked betwixt his house and Luxor, realising that he only had two clear weeks to prepare for Carnarvon's triumphant arrival. The archaeologist reminded his patron by cable that he should immediately apply for a new concession, for the discovery had taken place only four days within the limit of their present licence.

At his house Carter's canary seemed to erupt into ever more joyful song, as if it were in harmony with its master's euphoria. His domestic arrangements were thrown into reverse, for now the use of his house would become of paramount importance.

The boss gaffir, on Carter's instruction, immediately enrolled twenty extra workmen, who quickly set up camp, erecting more tents. The labour force began to clear the perimeter of the site, moving, in the process, many additional tons of rubble.

On 18 November Howard Carter took the night express to Cairo. The train rattled through the sleeping desert while the Englishman tossed and turned in fitful slumber, his subconscious preoccupied with thoughts of the coming day. He awoke to watch the ancients' golden disc arise from behind the sand dunes. The very air seemed to glow and he managed to shave by the laterals beams of the sun. The train slowed down as they approached the outskirts of the capital. Already the peasantry were nearing the end of their daily trek to the city, carrying their produce either on their heads or on the backs of donkeys.

Eventually the train clattered across the iron-built bridge, the lazy water of the Nile having long since passed through Luxor. Shortly Howard Carter was being jostled by the pressing throng in the madcap streets of Cairo. Traps, donkeys, dragomen, motor cars and camels intermingled in loud and strident confusion. The archaeologist set up his advance headquarters in Shepheard's Hotel and busied himself about his tasks, not the least of which was liaison with the Antiquities Department to advise and consult them on detail.

Three days later he was back at Luxor, followed on the 23rd by Lord Carnarvon and his daughter, Evelyn. The safe arrival of his patron was the signal for Carter's assistant, Callender, to set to work. Together with the boss gaffir he supervised the uncovering of the tomb.

On 24 November, in a state of hardly suppressed excitement, Carter informed the gaffir that a lady would be coming and that, therefore, the site must be made particularly clean. He and Callender descended to the bottom of the steps and it was at this moment, in the full light of the early morning sun, that Carter made yet another discovery. The fourteenth step was not, as he had thought, the bottom of the stairway. Two more remained, packed with sand and rubble. Working rapidly the two men began to excavate. Then, even as Carter was trowelling sand away from the plaster at the bottom of the doorway, his body suddenly stiffened and he let out an involuntary shout.

'Look,' he stabbed his finger at the plaster. Callender bent forward and Adamson, standing on the steps behind them, also looked down.

'Do you see?' Carter demanded of his astonished colleague. 'It's the cartouche of Tutankhamen!'

'My God!' Callender exclaimed.

But, almost in the instant, their premature hopes were dashed in bitter anti-climax. Standing back, Carter had detected a large patch of plaster that at some time had been cut out, then renewed. With almost a catch in his voice he murmured: 'We are not the first to have been here.'

There was utter silence as the two men contemplated the implacable evidence.

'But the repaired plaster bears the seal of the Necropolis,' Callender breathed. 'What can it mean?'

Photo: 'The Tim

Patrons and archaeologist: Lord Carnarvon and his daughter Evelyn – now a sprightly septuagenarian – and Howard Carter.

Carter said nothing. He had faced such disappointments before. He could do so again, but their burden did not lessen with the passing years, rather it grew.

'Perhaps they were disturbed . . .' he muttered to himself.

'You mean . . .'

'Tomb robbers, undoubtedly,' Carter said contemptuously.

'What ghastly bad luck.' Callender found voice to reply.

Photo: 'The Times'

Lord Carnarvon and Lady Evelyn drive out of the empty tomb pressed into service as a garage.

'Anyway it has been resealed; perhaps the contents are complete.'

Carter fetched his camera and took several photographs. It was shortly after lunch when the car arrived bearing Lord Carnarvon and Lady Evelyn Herbert. Again the camp bubbled with enthusiasm.

Carter went forward to greet them. A second vehicle came into view carrying two Egyptian Inspectors. After an exchange of greetings Carter introduced Adamson, who was standing nearby. Lord Carnarvon smiled affably.

'This is my man who has been looking after things up here.'

'Lady Evelyn Herbert,' his lordship introduced.

'I'm glad to meet you, my lady.' Adamson inclined his head.

She was dressed in a long black skirt, with a dark hat of contemporary fashion. She looked somewhat solemn, but yet managed a smile.

Lord Carnarvon was calm and remained ever more so as Carter's every movement betrayed his nervous emotions. Without more ado the archaeologist led the way to the steps. At the top he stood aside for his lordship, but Carnarvon motioned that he should precede them.

Ready in position, at the bottom, was a toolbag containing mallets, chisels and other equipment. At last the moment had come. Beckoning them forward Carter showed Carnarvon and his daughter the seals deeply impressed in the plaster. Next he pointed out the other puzzling features. In the final rubbish at the bottom of the stairway they had found broken potsherds and a scarab of Thothmes III, also a fragment of pottery with the name, Amenhetep III. Perhaps the tomb was merely a cache that had contained objects brought from Tel-el-Amarna by Tutankhamen himself.

The next task was to begin removal of the actual blocking of the door and, if possible, to preserve the seals intact.

Everyone retired, leaving Carter, Callender and the workmen

to proceed. Gradually, as the plaster came down, the beginning of a passage was revealed, tight packed with sand and rubble.

Another disappointment awaited them. Carter pointed out to Callender a darker patch of rubble at the top, left-hand side. Someone, over three thousand years before, had forced a tiny tunnel even through the rubble. Obviously, when refilled by the priests, a slightly differing selection of stones had been used. It augured ill. Now they must remove every stone in the passage.

Without more ado Carter and Callender made way for the Egyptian workers. Soon a double line of labourers were jostling up and down the stairway, their baskets bulging with rock chipping, their feet setting up small clouds of dust. The passage was seven feet high and six feet in width, and sloped at a steady rake downwards, but it had no steps. They toiled for the rest of the afternoon, while the party of onlookers above them tried their best to pass away the time. The further they burrowed the greater grew the tension. At last the day drew to a close.

The following morning work continued unabated, but further disappointments awaited them. Amongst the rubble Carter was now finding fragments of broken pottery, whole and broken alabaster jars, broken potsherds and water-skins that had been used in mixing the plaster. These tell-tale signs only underlined the fact that, without any doubt, the tomb had been plundered by robbers. Meanwhile Callender was constructing a massive wooden door to set at the mouth of the passage.

Thursday, 26 November. The passage now extended for a full thirty feet at which point, amidst the dust-laden atmosphere, Carter saw yet another door, similar to the first, now blocking their way. With his face encrusted with a fine layer of dust he struggled out of the airless passage to convey the news to Lord Carnarvon. Gradually, after what seemed an age, the final chipping and rubble was cleared. It was decided to sweep the passage and allow the dust to settle.

The party now took refreshment and began to tingle with excitement. What lay beyond? Carter informed them that, by

Lord Carnarvon, Lady Evelyn Herbert and Howard Carter at the top of the steps leading to the tomb. Already the idle and the curious were beginning to assemble. The stone wall was quickly erected to keep them at a distance.

Photo: 'The Times'

the light of his torch, he had seen more seals of Tutankhamen but, sadly, he reported again that the door had been broached. However, the repair work by the priests still bore the intact seals of the Necropolis.

As Carter and Callender sipped their glasses of lemon juice the former explained to their attentive listeners that, undoubtedly, they were about to find the remains of a cache. The question that burnt in his mind was how much of it had been plundered?

It was almost with a sense of reluctance that Carter got to his feet to test his faith in that which they had found. Again his nervousness began to assert itself and his movements became finicky and agitated in the extreme. He led the way down the

steps, passing from the blazing sunlight into the still, dust-laden gloom. He heard Lord Carnarvon catch his breath and begin to cough. The three torches they carried flicked across the walls, hand-chipped yet smooth. The boss gaffir was standing at the bottom awaiting them.

'The candles,' Carter muttered and sought them in the darkness. 'Where is the crowbar?'

The gaffir handed it to him. He was almost petulant as he demanded the equipment.

He sensed the others crowding in behind him, blocking out any vestige of light that might have permeated the darkness from the entrance. He grasped the crowbar and, with trembling hands, thrust it at the plaster in the top, left-hand corner. It was dry and crumbled. He pushed a little harder. It encountered some stone. Extracting it, he used the point to pull down more plaster. The rubble fell to the floor in a dull, angry rattle, as if the very gods were clearing their throats to roar their disapproval at this unforgivable intrusion. He lifted the crowbar once more, placed the point in the three-inch excavation, and thrust all his weight against it. It slipped right through, against what appeared to be no opposition. A void; a nothingness; a chamber.

A sudden flow of warm air beat against his face and he remembered the candles. Bending down, he grasped one, lit it, waited for the flame to develop, then held it high against the aperture. Its slender flame swooped and guttered, casting weird shadows across his sweat and dust-encrusted face. But the flame still burned brightly.

'At least the air is not foul,' he muttered, as if to himself.

With his free hand Carter began to pull at the masonry. It was dry and crumbled, unresisting, trickling down his front, on past his legs and accumulating round his feet. Lifting the candle again he pushed his hand through the hole. Still the warm air rushed at him and nearly extinguished the flame. He thrust his head to the opening. None of his companions dared breathe; not a sound disturbed the sepulchral silence. It was suddenly as if Carter had been turned to stone.

At first he could see absolutely nothing, the flame too close to his eyes. Then they adjusted and his companions heard him snatch his breath, as if in awe.

Out of the silence and blackness of three thousand years he began to see animals and statues and gold. He moved his hand to the left and then to right. He was struck dumb with amazement. It was a treasure-house, stuffed full of strange objects and animals, and everywhere the dull glint of gold.

Suddenly an eye seemed to glare back at him out of the darkness and he beheld the god Hathor, gold and black, standing in the form of a couch. Of a sudden he realised he could hear Lord Carnarvon calling, cutting through to his brain like a knife.

'Can you see anything?' his lordship exclaimed, for the second time of asking.

Carter fought for words of description.

'Yes,' he found himself saying. 'Wonderful things.'

Tearing away at still more masonry Carter widened the hole and then thrust in an electric torch. Now Lord Carnarvon pushed beside him, while tiny Lady Evelyn and Callender stood in wonderment, having waited impatiently in the darkness. Suddenly Lord Carnarvon remembered his daughter, pulled her forward, and she also beheld the sight that would remain imprinted on her memory for ever.

It was when Carter looked in for the second time that his academic brain began to make sense of that which he saw. As the beam of his torch again swept the chamber, it became riveted on two life-size statues that stood erect, untiring, contemptuous of the years, standing solemnly on sentinel duty. They must be the Royal Kas in which the king's spirit lived. Impassive, ebony black, kilted and gold sandalled, they were armed with staff and mace, while on their head-dresses a protective cobra sat frozen in gilt. They rigidly defied intrusion.

Carter had already noted that the chamber contained no sarcophagus. In a fleeting second his brain had untied the problem. He directed his torch to the wall in between the two statues. There, awaiting them, was yet another sealed doorway. Suddenly, with overwhelming force, the full significance of the situation burst in upon him. What he was looking at was only an antechamber. They were still but on the threshold of their discovery. Behind the wall must be the burial chamber of the pharaoh. Looking at the life-sized features of the king he marked how young he looked.

Neither Carter, nor Carnarvon, nor Lady Evelyn could take any more. They were all subdued, and moved back up the passage, suddenly conscious that they needed fresh air. They walked solemnly past Adamson who immediately took his turn at the peephole. He was equally staggered by the sight that met his gaze; his own impression, that he was looking through a golden mist at treasures untold.

Carter asked Callender to reseal the hole and next supervised the positioning of a crude, but heavy, wooden gate which his colleague had hastily constructed.

The party walked out into the unreality of the sunlit afternoon; the valley already becoming steeped in shadow. Nobody spoke, each lost in his own personal wonderment. Suddenly Carter turned to Adamson. 'Richard, this is only the beginning. You will have to remain on guard again tonight. Tomorrow I will arrange for extra police protection.'

This time the military policeman needed no explanation.

CHAPTER FIVE

PROPHETIC WARNING

As Lord Carnarvon, Lady Evelyn Herbert, Callender and Howard Carter began to wend their way back to Luxor the fires on the hillsides betokened some human habitation. The sun had departed, leaving the sky stained dark mauve and purple, yet only one evening star heralded the oncoming night.

For Lady Evelyn the experience of the afternoon would prove to be quite unforgettable. Even now the memory of her first impressions coursed through her brain. As she stood on the threshold of the antechamber the thought had occurred to her that, probably, one of the last people to leave the vault would have been the young king's widow. Now, after the passage of three thousand years, she, another woman from another time, had gazed on the selfsame scene. Even the very air she breathed may have been shared by the long dead queen. As her father had beckoned her in she had hesitated before taking her first steps into the chamber. In the deep silence, as she began to peer about her, Evelyn had been grateful that neither her father nor Carter were speaking. Had they done so it would have seemed an irreverence; but they were also caught up in the atmosphere and, but for an occasional exclamation, their examination was conducted in silence. Lady Evelyn noticed the queen's last gift of flowers, a token of love which, upon closer inspection, still bore a vestige of colour. When, eventually, they were about to leave the tomb Lord Carnarvon had turned to his daughter.

'Would you like to go in again, darling?'

'No, thank you,' she had replied very softly.

'Why not?' her father had countered in surprise.

'No, thank you, papa,' she avoided the question.

Evelyn wanted to retain for a lifetime the tranquillity and first memory of all she had seen.

Carter decided that, immediately he reached the Winter Palace Hotel, he would send a message to Engelbach, the Chief Inspector of the Antiquities Department, to advise him of the extent of their discovery and invite him to make an official inspection. Already it was obvious that the antechamber contained hundreds of priceless articles. These would have to be photographed, catalogued and preserved, even before they could be removed. He could already see months of work ahead, if not years. Howard Carter determined that he would resist all haste, for it would be his undeniable duty to posterity to record in meticulous fashion everything he had found.

Eventually they reached the Nile and took the ferry which transported them back to the twentieth century. It was not to Carter's liking.

At the Winter Palace Hotel they washed and changed, then enjoyed a leisurely dinner, thereafter sitting in the lounge talking into the early hours of the morning. It had been an exhilarating experience. Before them lay the practicalities. And what further discoveries?

Early the following day, denied much sleep, they set off again for the Valley of the Kings, now a still more meaningful name. One of their first requirements would be the supply of electric light and Callender set about laying temporary cables from the main lighting system, happily available in the valley.

While he was busy about this task, Carter and Lord Carnarvon decided to record the seals on the inner door of the antechamber. They trooped down the steps, fumbled in the gloom of the passage and came to the entrance of the chamber. Again the atmosphere proved quite overwhelming. Carter's torch picked out a half-filled bowl of mortar that had been used for sealing the door; then there was a smoke-blackened lamp that might have flickered flame but a day or two before. Here and there were fingermarks and, still most touching of all, the garland of flowers. They saw alabaster vases and caskets inlaid to perfection; chairs of great beauty, and couches, and a golden, inlaid throne that defied description; then, amidst the utter confusion, dismantled chariots and glittering harness.

Drawn, as if by a magnet, Carter and Carnarvon moved to the wall and gazed at the forms of his majesty. The statues stared back at him. Carter peered at the plaster wall and felt the disappointment surging within him again.

'Look,' he pointed his finger for Carnarvon. 'It's again been resealed. I wonder if they reached the king?'

They recorded the seals and then withdrew for counsel.

As they were sipping fresh lemon juice outside the tomb the local Antiquities Inspector, Ibraham Effendi, arrived in place of Engelbach who was temporarily absent. When Carter took him below the Egyptian stood in silent amazement, lost in incredulity at the treasures he saw, all fashioned by the hands of his distant ancestors.

It was a few hours later that Carter and Carnarvon reached a unanimous, if reluctant, decision. They decided that the inner door must remain sealed until all the contents of the antechamber had been catalogued, photographed, preserved and removed. The risk of damaging them would have been unthinkable. But Howard Carter allowed himself one personal quirk of superstition; he would leave the Royal Kas, the statues, until the very end to guard, he hoped, the body of the king. They had made two more important discoveries while in the chamber. The first, that nearly all the objects bore the name of Tutankhamen. Secondly they had noticed, when peering beneath one of the three great couches, a small, irregular hole in the wall. It had obviously once been sealed but, for some unknown reason, the priests had failed to repair it. Carter had managed to crawl to it on his hands and knees and, with the aid of his torch, had peered in. To his amazement he found yet another chamber, if possible even more crowded with objects than the one he was in. However, yet again, it had been ransacked from top to bottom. He felt a sudden, intense revulsion for those hands that had desecrated the tomb. Perhaps it could be said that he was intent on performing a similar task but, at least, it was in a spirit of reverence.

Both Carnarvon and Carter immediately agreed that they would need massive police protection for, not only as professional archaeologists but also as agents for the Egyptian government, they were responsible for the contents of the tomb. 'I think I'd better go to Cairo and supervise the making of a heavy metal gate which we can insert over the entrance to the antechamber,' Carter suggested and Lord Carnarvon agreed.

It was when they reached Luxor that night that they faced a new and unexpected problem that was about to cast a cloud over all their future activities. By that indefinable bush telegraph, word had already got round of their spectacular discovery. When they entered the lobby of the hotel they were besieged by throngs of excited people. The Winter Palace was positively seething with speculation and rumour. One story already had it that three aeroplanes had been seen to land in the valley, load up with treasure and depart to destinations unknown! By what superhuman act of aviational skill this could have been achieved was a point the rumour-mongers forgot to mention. Nevertheless, the story was to wing its way across the world.

For the first time Carnarvon became anxious, for his and Carter's reputations might well be at stake. He determined that, as a first precautionary move, they would immediately invite Lord and Lady Allenby to an official opening.

He also deemed it politic to suggest to *The Times* newspaper's local correspondent that he might like to witness the event and send an authoritative despatch back to England. In the event it was unfortunate that Lord Allenby, presently wrestling with the political unrest, would himself be unable to attend but, appreciating the significance of the occasion, he agreed that his wife should represent him and, accordingly, she travelled down to Luxor.

On 29 November Lady Allenby, Abd el Aziz Bey Yehia, the Governor of the Province, and Mohamed Bey Fahmy, Mamour of the district, plus several other Egyptian officials, together with Mr Merton of *The Times*, were conducted into the tomb of Tutankhamen by Howard Carter. However, on this occasion, he stopped short at the entrance to the antechamber, only allowing his guests to peer in.

As the official party had neared the entrance to the tomb Lady Allenby had suddenly caught sight of Richard Adamson. Immediately a look of recognition had flashed in her eyes. Smiling she walked across to him.

'Don't I recognise you from the residency?'

'Yes, my lady. I was on your staff for three years.'

'I thought so,' she laughed. 'How do you like it up here?'

'It's a little bit different to Cairo, my lady, but we have had our excitements.'

The following morning *The Times* splashed Merton's story, by-lined:

FROM OUR CAIRO CORRESPONDENT: VALLEY OF THE KINGS BY RUNNER TO LUXOR. It was headed: AN EGYPTIAN TREASURE. GREAT FIND AT THEBES. LORD CARNARVON'S LONG QUEST.

This historic despatch veritably set the world on fire with curiosity.

It was perhaps fortunate that Carnarvon and Carter, in agreement with the local Egyptian officials, decided that, until they were ready to commence operations, they must seal up the tomb and refill the steps with rubble, right to the surface. Only by that method would they feel that the tomb was totally secure, in spite of the presence of Adamson. Nothing less would suit Carter while he went to Cairo to handle the massive preparations. For the time being, there was nothing else he could do in Luxor.

On 4 December Lord Carnarvon and Lady Evelyn embarked on their triumphant return to England. Many practical and legal arrangements had to be put in hand in London. They would return in the early New Year.

It was on the very evening of the day that *The Times* had splashed Merton's story that Count Louis Hamon and his wife were sitting alone in their new home in the West End of London. No doubt subconsciously influenced by the publication of the story, they fell to discussing, for the first time since their arrival back in England, their experience when cremating the hand of the mummy.

They were sitting in Hamon's study and his wife took out a sketch book and began to try to re-create from memory the features of the supposed Princess Makitaten. She was almost at the point of completing her sketch when they suddenly noticed that the light from the bulbs in their room was beginning to fade. The lamp on the desk diminished to a dull, red glow. Even before they could say anything, and to their complete incredulity, the image of the princess began to reappear. It seemed vague and ephemeral, but her hand appeared to be pointing at the desk.

Hamon looked in the direction indicated and saw his scribbling pad. Instinctively he seized a pencil and found himself writing. Suddenly, in the space of only a few seconds, the vision began to fade and the lights returned to normal. He looked down to read the words he had written:

LORD CARNARVON NOT TO ENTER TOMB. DIS-OBEY AT PERIL. IF IGNORED WOULD SUFFER SICKNESS; NOT RECOVER; DEATH WOULD CLAIM HIM IN EGYPT.

Cheiro was so affected and convinced of the well-meaning intention of the warning that he immediately penned a letter to Lord Carnarvon at Highclere Castle.

Feeling secure in the knowledge that Callender would look after the Luxor end, Howard Carter took the train to Cairo. His first task would be to order the manufacture of the heavy steel gates which would secure the safety of the inner tomb. Delivery was promised within six days.

For his part, Callender was to supervise the enrolment of additional labour and to earmark certain of the nearby tombs to provide space for a preservation laboratory, storerooms, and a small photographic 'dark room'. Callender slipped between the valley and Luxor, whereas Adamson remained permanently on site.

No sooner had Merton's report been published in *The Times* than an ever-increasing daily flow of visitors began to invade the valley. Arrangements were immediately made for a detachment of local Egyptian police to make a post at the entrance to the valley. From this moment it was decided that it would be politic for Adamson to wear only civilian attire.

It was while staying in Shepheard's Hotel that Howard Carter received a telegram from Albert Lythgoe, Curator of the Egyptian Department of the Metropolitan Museum of Art, New York. He was presently excavating another site just over the mountain wall at Thebes. In a magnanimous gesture, which brooked no jealousy, he offered the complete support of his own expedition. A generous man by nature, he had on hand specialists in a variety of fields, not least of whom was Harry Burton, a photographer of the highest possible calibre. Other offers of help poured in. Dr Alan Gardiner undertook to deal with all inscriptional material and Professor Breasted agreed to help decipher the historic significance of the seals they were finding.

In addition to these beneficial demonstrations of support another phenomena began to occur. Lord Carnarvon, *en route* to England, Howard Carter in Cairo, and Callender and Adamson in Luxor suddenly found themselves besieged by the international press. The fact that Luxor was four hundred and fifty miles up Nile from the capital seemed to present no problems to a host of journalists, who sped to Egypt by every means possible from all corners of the world. Each newspaper was vying, one against the other, to learn the significance of the find and add, if possible, to the already authoritative statement by Merton in *The Times.*

By now, of course, his lordship and Lady Evelyn were aboard the S.S. *Kaiser-i-Hind* and were temporarily, at least, removed from the general harassment they had received from the press. However *The Times* badly needed a follow-up story and so despatched a special correspondent to Marseilles.

When the ship docked on 17 December, he boarded it and sought an interview. His report stated:

> Lord Carnarvon talked in a calm and matter-of-fact way of the romantic discoveries made by himself and Mr Howard Carter in the Valley of the Kings and, with quiet confidence, of what the future may reveal.
>
> 'We are resigned to the necessity of waiting,' Lord Carnarvon said. 'The wall barring the way to the inner chamber cannot be touched without serious risk to the valuable antiquities scattered in indescribable confusion in the outer chamber.'

The despatch continued:

> There remains the mystery of the north wall of the outer chamber, jealously guarded by the two gigantic, bitumenised statues of King Tutankhamen. They stand, life-size, one in the north-east corner and the other in the north-west corner. The figures are not adorned with elaborately dressed beards, such as one is accustomed to seeing in representations of kings of Ancient Egypt. They are probably authentic portraits of the king. Standing erect, holding in one hand a gold stick and in the other a mace, the costume is a tunic of the period. The handsome features, with eyes of glass, are crowned with an elaborate head-dress studded with gems. The feet are enclosed in shoes with a ring of metal that may prove to be gold.
>
> In the centre of the north wall, between these statues, is

the closed entrance to a chamber, or a series of chambers, beyond it. Lord Carnarvon is convinced that, in all human probability, the tomb of King Tutankhamen lies beyond the wall.

'If that assumption is justified,' Lord Carnarvon added, with an emphasis which portrayed his faith in this prophecy, 'then when the wall gives up its secret the revelation will be stupendous.'

After thirty years' patient, if unrecognised, work in Egypt Howard Carter had become the focal point of the news media of the world. At this moment it was a curious, almost pleasurable, experience but it was not to remain so for long.

In London a newspaper interview was given by the noted Egyptologist, Professor Flinders Petrie, with whom Howard Carter had worked on his first visit to Egypt in 1892. He made two significant observations.

The first, that he pronounced himself: '. . . as highly gratified at the success which has attended Mr Carter's efforts. Mr Carter's long experience in this sort of work was a guarantee that the objects discovered would be looked after with all the care that is necessary in the preservation of such valuable articles of antiquity.' This was a most gracious and, indeed, accurate compliment which would have a bearing on the future.

'It is evident,' continued Petrie, 'that one of the full-sized royal tombs, with several chambers, has been discovered.'

With regard to the suggested robbery of the tomb, Professor Petrie said that the famous Abbott Papyrus and documents concerned with the robberies of the royal tombs gave a full account of the attack on the tombs in the reign of Rameses X and the trial of thieves.

'It looks,' he added, 'as if the tomb now discovered has been robbed of all the gold. Apparently there are no precious metals left, except the surface gilding.'

This was a somewhat premature conclusion for, on the same day, a Reuter's report commented: 'Egyptologists describe the discovery as beyond the dreams of avarice and value it at millions of pounds sterling.'

The next tribute to be published was of Lord Carnarvon, by Sir Ernest Wallis Budge, Keeper of Egyptian and Assyrian Antiquities at the British Museum. After a detailed and glowing account of the determined efforts by Carnarvon and Carter he made a final and significant observation.

'One other point needs mention. The laws which governed excavations made by foreigners in Egypt used to allot to the excavator one half of the find. Under Maspero these laws were generously interpreted, and all must hope that such will be the case in respect of the present discovery. Very valuable gifts were made to Mr Theodore Davis in return for the toil and money which he spent in excavating royal tombs, and we hope that Monsieur M. Lacau, the Director of the Cairo Museum, will follow the example of Maspero in his dealing with Lord Carnarvon. After all the labourer is worthy of his hire, but Lord Carnarvon has worked for sixteen years for nothing and spent money besides. England may congratulate herself that, even in these days of the "Axe", men can be found willing and magnanimous enough to spend treasure merely with the idea of increasing the sum of human knowledge.'

Upon his arrival in England, Lord Carnarvon, in his accustomed, unruffled calm, took everything in his stride. There were requests for interviews with the press; telephone calls from the academics of the British Museum; applications by the score from those would-be treasure seekers wishing to join the enlarged expedition; even inquiries from manufacturers, who offered equipment to make him the more able to find gold and treasure!

But lastly, and far more disquieting, was the letter he had received from Count Hamon. It was well known that the Ancient Egyptians performed magic rites to guard their sleeping pharaohs but, in all the years that he had been concerned with excavation, no personal dilemma had ever confronted him.

Carnarvon happened to know the seer and palmist, Velma, and he decided to seek his advice rather than consult directly with Cheiro. Velma was famed for many predictions, including the assassination of the tsar of Russia and his son, Alexis Nicolaevitch, and the death of Francisco Pancho-Villa, the bandit and Mexican President, whose hand he had read on the outskirts of Mexico City. Possibly one of the most significant, recorded prophecies he made was to the then duchess of York.* He met her at an Elizabethan Pageant in aid of charity at Hatfield, the ancestral home of the Cecils.

Velma had been provided with a booth in the Elizabethan gipsy encampment. Amidst a flutter of excitement the young duchess, accompanied by some friends, arrived at his stall. Laughingly she held out her hand.

It was somewhat spatulate in shape, indicating her descent from feudal barons. The Line of Life showed on both hands, strong and clear, indicating long life. A line extending from the Mount of Venus to that of Mercury indicated great capacity for loyalty and affection. The Line of Saturn started from the Life Line, indicating good fortune through personal merit. The Head Line was joined to the Life Line, sharply left it, and proceeded directly to the Mount of Moon without interruption. This indicated good sense, clear and strong willpower.

'Then you consider that I have a very good hand?' inquired the duchess with a smile. 'Is that all you have to tell me?'

'Well, your royal highness,' Velma replied, 'there are several other features in your hand which are all of good omen, but which it is difficult for me to speak to you of in detail.'

'Do tell me if it is anything interesting,' the duchess begged.

Velma looked hard at the palm again.

'I see by indications on the various lines and mounts of your hand that your marriage, so happy and successful, will be made more successful still by the arrival of a child who will be worshipped from one end of the Empire to the other. You are, at the present time, in a mansion that stood in Elizabethan times and this is an Elizabethan Fête. It may well be that all the great

* Now. of course, H.M. Elizabeth the Queen Mother.

characteristics of the queen of that name will be found in the princess of your house. She may even be of as great importance in the history of the country. That she will be an influence for good is guaranteed by her parentage. This is the crown of your happiness.'

The duchess continued to smile with a look upon her face which seemed to declare, 'Who knows?'*

When Lord Carnarvon visited Velma he explained the warning letter he had received and, stretching forth his hands, asked the palmist to read them. Velma knew of Carnarvon's interest in the occult and also that he believed in palmistry. He found a fairly long Life Line, but thin in the centre, where there was an ominous spot which – given other combinations in the hand – might indicate death. Unfortunately it seemed that the confirming signs were there also, for there was a spot at the junction of the Lines of Heart and Apollo. This indicated a great peril, from which, probably, the possessor of the hand would not permit his head to turn him. The Line of Apollo denoted great glory and success. More than ordinary interest in occult matters was indicated by the fact that the Health Line was forked at the Head Line.

Velma paused and looked up.

'I do see great peril for you,' he confirmed. 'Most probably – as the indications of occult interest are so strong in your hand – it will arise from such a source.'

Lord Carnarvon made a spirited, in-character reply. 'Whatever happens I will see to it that my interest in things occult never gets so strong as to affect either my reason or my health.'

Although putting a brave face on it Carnarvon left in sombre mood.

Even Adamson's lone vigil at the tomb was disturbed by newspapermen of all nationalities, who were descending by all means possible on the remote little valley in the Theben hills.

* The report of this meeting and prediction was published in 1929.

In the hearts of all the English journalists there was a burning desire to grasp back the initiative won by *The Times*. Adamson became the focal point of their attention but, before Carter had left for Cairo, he had already instructed him: 'Say absolutely nothing. You don't know anything and, therefore, you have nothing to say.'

This, as might be expected, did not satisfy the legions of correspondents.

When Carter arrived back from Cairo he was carrying a batch of international newspapers and he addressed himself with some asperity to the military policeman: 'What have you been doing talking to the *Sunday X*?'

Adamson was fairly nonplussed by the attack. 'I haven't been talking to the *Sunday X*. You told me not to. In fact, when the reporter came down, I referred him to you.'

Carter thrust forward a copy of the offending article. It was a long despatch published on 3 December. Having, in the first paragraph, recognised the sensational achievement of Lord Carnarvon and Howard Carter, it put a price on the treasures as yet unseen.

'They are valued at three million pounds,' the reporter informed his readers. Not content with that they had even published an engraving which boldly, if recklessly, they captioned 'Tutankhamen'. Of course, the illustration was wrong. How could it be anything else with the wall into the burial chamber still standing intact.

'If you remember, Mr Carter, I referred the reporter to you and he attended your briefing.'

Carter fell silent. Reports like these were incensing the academic sensibilities of the archaeologist. After Adamson's rebuttal of the charge Carter seemed somewhat mollified but, looking about him at the idle knots of people gazing from the periphery of the camp, some of whom at least must have been journalists, he muttered: 'Something is going to have to be done about this,' with which sentiment Adamson ardently agreed.

D

Overnight fame was one thing, but streams of news-hungry journalists descending on the valley at all hours of the day and night, many offering bribes, others demanding information by right, was a situation that very soon palled. As it happened the *Sunday X* journalist was a very nice man and was only intent on his job. Richard Adamson made a mental note to be even more wary of such charms in the future.

In Cairo the manufacture of the steel gates had been completed and, with the cooperation of the Egyptian State Railway, they and the rest of the items purchased by Howard Carter were sent south to Luxor by express, rather than by normal freight train.

On 16 December the rubble was again removed from the entrance to the tomb and, on the following day, the steel gates were manœuvred down the passage to the entrance of the chamber, where they were secured with iron bars and bolts.

Harry Burton, the American photographer, duly arrived and set up his dark-room equipment in the unnamed tomb which had once held the cache of objects brought by the Pharaoh Akhenaten, from Tel-al-Amarna.

Almost immediately upon his return to Luxor Howard Carter met his old friend, Winlock, working on the Metropolitan Museum excavation. It was he who had released Harry Burton and now offered the additional services of two more members of his expedition, Messrs Hall and Hauser, his key draughtsmen. In addition Arthur Mace, Director of the Metropolitan's excavations on the Pyramid field at Lisht, also agreed to join Carter and shortly arrived in the valley. This made a total of four invaluable colleagues, the services of whom were donated by the trustees and director of the Metropolitan Museum, New York. Lastly, on 20 December, the Director of the Chemical Department of the Egyptian Government, Mr Lucas, reported to the site. He was about to retire and had just started three months' leave of absence before returning to England. However, he had offered his assistance to Carter in Cairo, who had been delighted to accept! Lucas' knowledge of preservation techniques would be invaluable. Their team was now all but ready.

However, as the first shovels began to remove the chipping and rubble from the entrance the press erupted in full cry, demanding that, before the archaeologists set to work, they must be allowed an inspection of the tomb and a full-scale briefing. Carter sent a message to Carnarvon in London and also contacted the local authorities. Lord Carnarvon cabled his immediate agreement to the demand.

On 21 December a massive throng of pressmen crowded into the marquee to listen to Carter and his assistant, Callender, describe the background to the discovery and the contents of the antechamber.

Later, in small groups, they were conducted down the steps into the passage, but only as far as the doorway, now safely secured by the steel gate. Then followed a general stampede by donkey cart, pony, or simply on foot, as the journalists fought to be first to reach the end of the telephone line at Luxor.

In London the Court Circular announced:

> The king received Lord Carnarvon in audience at Buckingham Palace yesterday and listened with great interest to a description of the important discoveries made recently by him and Mr Howard Carter as the culmination of the excavations which they have carried on for nearly sixteen years. Lord Carnarvon assured the king of his confident expectation that still further objects of great importance would be found when the third sealed chamber, believed to be the actual tomb of King Tutankhamen, is opened.

Yet a third public statement was issued on that day; this time from the government in Cairo and it bore ill tidings for the future.

> Regarding the ultimate fate of the treasure the ministry states that there is nothing to disturb the Egyptian public opinion and points out that, although regulations provide

that the discoverer should receive one half of the objects found, with the exception of certain articles which the Egyptian government reserves for itself, the Ministry of Public Works, knowing the archaeological importance of the zone of the Valley of the Kings, expressly provided in Lord Carnarvon's licence that he should have no right to any objects which he might find. The ministry adds that Lord Carnarvon willingly accepted this condition, which is the clear proof of his disinterestedness in the service of science and art.

In view of the large number of inquiries from intending visitors, in consequence of Lord Carnarvon's discoveries at Luxor, the Egyptian government officially announces that absolute tranquillity prevails throughout Egypt and that entirely adequate arrangements have been made by the authorities for the comfort of the visitors.

However a local Arabic newspaper printed the following:

It is the duty of the Egyptian government worthily and generously to reward, in the name of the whole nation, Lord Carnarvon and his devoted collaborators by offering Lord Carnarvon the highest honours, by reserving for the treasures discovered by him special rooms in the museum, by inscribing his name over the entrance to these rooms, and by erecting to him a statue as a sign of national gratitude and perpetuation of his name, and by awarding pecuniary and honorary rewards to his collaborators, particularly Mr Howard Carter.

Even as Howard Carter fought with the innumerable questions posed him by the press the dark clouds of politics and bureaucracy were mounting on the far horizon. These were not the only clouds to threaten the security of the Royal Valley of the Kings for, as occasionally happens at this season of the year, black rain clouds mounted in the otherwise azure sky. When a tropical downpour does occur in the area the waters collect

A young Howard Carter in an early motor-car at the Mena House Hotel, near the Great Pyramid.

in immeasurable force off the slopes of the mountains and then gush down in the form of a raging torrent, straight through the valley and out on to the Theben plain. Carter was almost beside himself with anxiety. Now that the steps and passage of the tomb had been cleared, if that elemental event should occur, nothing on earth would prevent the flooding of the chambers. He could only watch and pray.

Callender had built a stone wall round the parapet of the tomb and, in addition, the valley was now guarded throughout the twenty-four hours by three different groups of watchmen; the Government Antiquities Guard, a detachment of soldiers provided by the Mudir of Kena, together with Sergeant Richard Adamson who was entrusted with the keys of the metal gate. It was genuinely believed that, following the reports of the vast wealth of treasure expected to be found, an attempt by a modern team of tomb robbers could possibly be made at any time. Two days prior to Christmas, Carter shut the tomb to all visitors and began to put in hand final arrangements for the preservation and removal of the items in the antechamber, with the help of his formidable team of professionals.

As the task of emptying the tomb was about to begin the following letter was published in *The Times*:

Sir. Rarely have readers been so enthralled by contemporary literature as by the articles in your columns on Lord Carnarvon's discoveries in the Valley of the Kings. Especially fascinating was the story of that phenomenal personage, the saintly Akhenaton, who in dim, distant ages approximated so closely to a knowledge of the true and living God. It is hard enough, even in this twentieth century of the Christian era, to live according to the Golden Rule. What must it have been for a pharaoh thirteen hundred years before Christ? There are many who venture to hope that, after the legitimate claims of science and archaeology have been satisfied, it may be possible, in a spirit of pious regard for the religious convictions of the departed, to restore to their tombs the pathetic remains of those who, with many prayers and tears, were laid to their eternal rest.

With this sentiment Carter fully approved.

It was with something of a shock that late in the afternoon of 25 December 1922, the excavators paused in their tasks, realising that it was Christmas Day. Due to their intense preparations for emptying the antechamber the fact had escaped them.

On 26 December a much needed element of humour found space in the publication, *Al Mokattan*. It was a letter signed by a Dr Athanasius, a Copt, living in Old Cairo. He declared that he was in possession of certain papyri which proved his direct lineage from Tutankhamen and that he would take legal action forthwith against the government and anyone else unless his rights were recognised.

In London Lord Carnarvon was beginning to contemplate his return to Egypt. But, truth to tell, he was now becoming a very worried man. He decided to revisit Velma.

It was a cold, inhospitable day, in deep contrast to the weather in the valley, when he called at the palmist's chambers.

'I have been thinking over what you told me last time. I wonder if you can discover any more?'

So saying he sat down and proffered his hands to Velma.

To the palmist's considerable surprise he noticed that the ominous spots to which he had previously referred looked, if anything, as if they had increased in intensity. In particular, the spot on the Life Line seemed perilously close to the earl's present age.

He suggested that Carnarvon might like to look into his crystal. This he did, and stared at it for some little time, but what he saw was not very clear.

'I see something like a temple,' his Lordship stated, 'and there are people, but it is all so cloudy that I cannot make it out.'

Velma then took the crystal himself and began his concentration. He had no difficulty. He saw what appeared to be a great Egyptian temple, thronged with people divided into three separate parties. Picture followed picture, making this clear and, as they passed through the sphere, he described them to Lord Carnarvon.

'There is an old man robed as a dignitary of the Goddess Isis, who seems to be wrangling with a party of younger men who hold aloft a banner with hieroglyphics on it.'

From the mist which kept shrouding the figures came out the words, in English: 'To Aton . . . only God . . . Universal Father . . .'

The mystery heightened when the scene changed to a spectacle of huge, sacred bulls and priests singing a dirge, while the old dignitary placed a mask of gold over the face of a young man in a coffin.

Velma looked up for a moment.

'Nothing says so, but I believe that this is the burial of your King Tutankhamen.'

He looked down again and the picture changed. Suddenly he saw Lord Carnarvon working in the vicinity. From a mysterious tomb began to come vivid flashes, a sure sign of occult influences. As Lord Carnarvon and his party continued their work the flashes increased in vividness. The series of pictures ended in an amazing spectacle. The old dignitary again appeared, surrounded by a great concourse of people who demanded vengeance against the disturbers of the tomb. Then, finally, Lord Carnarvon was standing alone in the very storm centre of a hurricane of occult flashing.

The pictures faded and there was silence in the salon. Lord Carnarvon was the first to speak.

'Of course it all sounds ridiculous, but I have actually experienced some strange influence during the earlier stages of this work. I cannot say that it was actually an impulse to stop, but it was something like that. But no one would jib at an adventure even if there is danger. Having gone so far with the work my curiosity and interest must be satisfied now.'

Velma studied his client carefully.

'If I were you,' he suggested quietly, 'I should make some public excuse and finish. I can only see disaster to you, without any adequate gain to humanity to justify the sacrifice.'

Carnarvon shook his head. 'That is out of the question. Why, if I were to give up there are a hundred men waiting to step into my shoes. Oh no, I must finish what I have begun.'

Lord Carnarvon shrugged his shoulders and laughed. 'Tell me, Velma, what do you think is the real answer to all this mysterious business? Is it preposterous rot to think of all these priests still surviving today?'

Velma replied immediately.

'Wherever a place has been the focus of tremendous emotion

there is not the slightest doubt that something – I don't know what – persists.'

'I'm rather inclined to agree with you,' Lord Carnarvon said seriously.

Then he ended with a characteristic smile. 'But what an adventure; a challenge to the psychic powers of the ages!'

CHAPTER SIX

THE TABERNACLE

O n 27 December the Exchange Telegraph Company sent this report from Luxor:

The removal of the contents of the tomb of Tutankhamen to the outer passage of the tomb of Seti II was begun this morning. As the work is very delicate progress was limited today to the removal of two articles. The first was a magnificent, inlaid box, containing sandals and slippers, rich jewellery, a wonderful black amber necklace, the Queen's robes, and other objects which are still buried under the objects enumerated. The second was a huge alabaster vase, containing a black substance.

But Howard Carter was beginning to become exasperated. Sightseers and journalists could now be numbered in hundreds and matters were coming to such a pass that there was a distinct danger of damage to the treasures as they were being transported from the tomb to the laboratory. Carter communicated his fears to Carnarvon in London in no uncertain terms. Something had to be done.

Lord Carnarvon hit upon a solution which was to earn the expedition much unpopularity. He contacted *The Times* newspaper, agreeing in principle to an earlier suggestion that they might handle the dissemination of all information on an exclusive basis, for which privilege they would be prepared to pay a nominal sum of some several thousand pounds. A bargain was sealed, to the outraged fury of every competitive newspaper throughout the world. Three people became victims of their wrath: Howard Carter, Adamson, and Merton, the local *Times* correspondent, whose despatches had been regaling the reading public of Britain.

To relieve the pressure on Merton, Carter suggested that he should remain at the Winter Palace Hotel in Luxor, where the archaeologist would brief him each night.

Adamson, in true Yorkshire style, had to battle it out alone, being as polite and inoffensive as possible, but constantly heckled and harried by the caustic comments of the journalists.

'It's simply not good enough.'

'This is damned unfair.'

'We'll see about this.'

'We'll complain to the Egyptian authorities.'

On several occasions he only just avoided a set-to with fisti-cuffs. Only *The Times* and Lord Carnarvon appeared unruffled.

Now, each day in the Valley of the Tombs of the Kings, there was enacted a solemn ritual. As the boss gaffir assembled his men, Carter and Callender would arrive at the entrance to the tomb and Adamson would produce the keys. Behind the parapet wall lined up the legions of onlookers, eyes agog, cameras at the ready, awaiting the dramas of the day.

At irregular intervals Carter and his workers would emerge from the tomb, like badgers from their sett, blinking their eyes in the glare of the sun. They could be carrying an alabaster vase or some portion of a stately royal couch. 'Oos' and 'Ahs' would echo through the valley as they made their way through the throng to the laboratory. Thereafter the crowd would subside in happy resignation, awaiting the next object to feast their eyes upon.

One American Travel Agency was already offering a package tour holiday to Luxor, to include a view of the excavation.

This, of course, was not the first time the valley had seen the tourist. The Greeks and Romans had been there before them. For instance, Dionysios and Poseidonax had visited the valley from Marseilles; while another inscription stated that Apollophanes, of Lycopolis, had visited the tombs in the seventh year of Antoninus. But it was a Roman official named Januarius who brought his daughter, Januarina, who left the words 'Saw and marvelled,' ending 'Valete omnes' imprinted in the rock.

A somewhat longer inscription read: 'I, Philastrios, the Alexandrian, who have come to Thebes and who have seen with mine eyes the work of these tombs of astounding horror, have spent a delightful day.'

How many of these Greeks and Romans had walked atop the tomb of Tutankhamen, little knowing of the treasures that lay beneath their feet? Even Napoleon's archaeologists had visited the Royal Valley.

But the tourists of 1922 were enjoying and marvelling at a unique experience.

It was on an evening of the first week in January that Howard Carter casually turned to Richard Adamson and said: 'There's enough room for you to take your bed down to the chamber now, Richard,' an instruction he issued in such centurion tones that they brooked no argument. Adamson merely nodded.

At dusk, when work had ceased for the day, leaving only Carter and Callender fussing in the laboratory amidst their treasures, the policeman carried down his trestle camp-bed and erected it, with some care, in the antechamber. He took down three blankets, some magazines and a book.

After a final look around outside and having said a pointed 'Good night' to Carter, he descended the steps, walked on down the passage and pulled the steel gate behind him. He clipped fast the padlock, turned the key and began to undress. He decided that, in the closeness of the atmosphere, pyjama bottoms were quite sufficient. Brushing the dust from his feet he lay down atop the blankets and began to read. Not a sound, not a mouse, not a beetle disturbed his concentration. The air seemed quite sweet and soon he became drowsy. In the last few moments of his consciousness he decided to leave the light burning.

It was at 4 a.m. that he awakened, for no reason other than he had gone to sleep too early. Try as he may he could not return to his slumber. He looked at the articles spread all around him. What on earth was he doing here, locked amidst this storehouse of treasure?

He suddenly felt conscious of the two statues that stood silently watchful behind him. He got up, slipped on his shoes, and went to investigate. There was something uncanny about them. Their features seemed tranquil, assured, yet commanding, and Carter had forbidden their removal. He allowed a finger to press gently the beaten gold of their headdress. It still shone with no imperfection. They were so still and lifelike, as if determined to resist any aggressor. He examined the other treasures and marvelled at the intricacy of their design. He went back to bed, cushioned his head on the pillow and wondered deeply if, behind the two statues, there really was a pharaoh sleeping.

He awakened when he heard someone coming down the steps. It was Callender and he was ready to start work.

'Did you sleep well?' he inquired, laughing, as Adamson threw on his clothes preparatory to making a hurried exit.

That evening Carter held his usual conference in the marquee when, for the benefit of everyone, he gave a résumé of the events of the day. At the end he invited questions. For the first and last time Adamson had the temerity to speak amidst the academics, steeped in their scholarship.

'Those two big statues, sir; what are they, and why don't you move them?'

Carter looked at him benignly.

'They are the Royal Kas, the abode of the pharaoh's soul, Richard. They became the refuge for the soul during the period of mummification. It is within those statues that it was believed the pharaoh still lived.'

Being a Yorkshireman and a straightforward soldier, Adamson's reply escaped before bidden. 'It would have been a queer old surprise if I had awoken to find one of them bending over me!'

The marquee erupted in laughter. Adamson went scarlet and vowed that he would never ask another damnfool question.

It was the following day that he had another serious clash with the gentlemen of the press. They were trying, by all means possible, to obtain an interview with Howard Carter, but the archaeologist remained adamant in his refusal. His only information would come via *The Times*.

'Just keep them away,' he instructed Adamson.

On this particular occasion he had stood his ground against almost fifty newsmen. One of them politely offered to knock off his head. The Yorkshireman retaliated: 'All right then. Come and try it.'

And when there seemed a general move in his direction he added, with alacrity: 'Not fifty at once, you bastards, just one at a time.'

Disgusted, they marched off, muttering abuse. Later he tried more soothing tactics and endeavoured to reason with them. 'Look, for God's sake, it's not my fault. Lord Carnarvon has made the arrangements in London. Mr Carter can't see you and he's told me to make it plain. Be good fellows and leave us to get on with the work.'

Then the photographers set about Burton, offering him riches untold if he would slip them one or two of his photographic plates. They got short shrift from the American, but he remained charming and conciliatory at all times. After all, they were his colleagues, and he respected that they were only doing their job.

But probably the worst one affected was Arthur Merton himself. He was the local representative of *The Times* and, on several occasions, almost came to blows with his competitors. These, it should be said, were not, in the main, the British correspondents who understood the vagaries of Fleet Street, but rather the representatives of the overseas press.

'Pecky' Callender, as Carter called him, bore the brunt of the work, relieving Carter of much of the strain. He organised, administered, and worked alongside the senior archaeologist. The days of January sped.

Lord Carnarvon and Lady Evelyn Herbert duly arrived back in Egypt, but Adamson quickly noticed a change. Although just as charming and urbane as ever it seemed to the military policeman that Lord Carnarvon's enthusiasm had abated. He appeared distant, unconcerned, as if, already in the finding, his part of the task had been completed.

It was by the end of the second week in February that, at last, after seven hard weeks, the antechamber was finally emptied. However, Carter still refused to allow the Kas to be removed. For their safety he had cocooned them in protective wrappings, but their sentinel duty he left them to perform. It was strange. On several occasions Adamson had entered the tomb when Carter was working alone. Walking down quietly, so as not to disturb him, he had heard the archaeologist talking, although no one was present. It was, with something of a shock, that he realised that the Englishman was holding conversation with either the spirit of the pharaoh, or the priests who had sealed the tomb. It was uncanny and Adamson came to suspect that Carter must believe in reincarnation.

Suddenly all talk revolved on the Sepulchral Chamber, and word swept round that Field-Marshal Lord Allenby, his wife, and the queen of the Belgians would attend the ceremony of its opening. Callender busied himself with putting the camp in order, smartening it up with the help of the Egyptian workers, while Adamson fought his losing battle with the multitude of tourists. Some of them, by now, were even camping out at night, either in tents or taking shelter in empty and disused tombs. He could often hear their whispered conversations in the darkness.

By the morning of Friday, 17 February, word had passed round Luxor of Lord Allenby's visit for the opening and, by dawn, people were beginning to arrive in hundreds. They came on donkeys, on horseback, in sand-carts, or two-horse cabs; and struggled for a good position at the wall.

The legend of this man had been born many years before and had been cemented when he captured Jerusalem from the Turks in 1917. The advance guard had entered the city and a sergeant in the Infantry had captured the keys of the city.

'These will have to be formally surrendered to General Allenby,' he told the Turkish officer concerned. The ceremony was arranged for the following morning. General Allenby and his staff-officers rode at the head of his troops until they reached the Jaffa Gate. On an impulse, remembering the entry of Jesus into the city on the back of a donkey, the Commander-in-Chief dismounted and walked on foot to St David's Hotel, where he accepted the surrender from the Turkish mayor.

At mid-day staff from the Winter Palace Hotel began to erect a generous outside buffet for the guests. Egyptian police patrolled the perimeter, immaculate and important, as befitted the occasion.

At the last minute Adamson was informed that Lord and Lady Allenby and the queen of the Belgians would, in fact, make their inspection on the following day. Friday, it had been decided, should, in the main, be set aside for prominent archaeologists.

As the appointed time of two o'clock drew near, the guests foregathered at the top of the steps. Lord Carnarvon; Lady Evelyn Herbert; his Excellency Abd el Halim Pasha Suleman, Minister of Works; M. Lacau, Director-General of the Service of Antiquities; Sir William Garstin; Sir Charles Cust; Mr Albert Lythgoe, Curator of the Egyptian Department of the Metropolitan Museum, New York; Professor Breasted; Dr Alan Gardiner; Mr Winlock; the Honourable Mervyn Herbert; the Honourable Richard Bethell; Mr Engelbach, Chief Inspector of the Department of Antiquities; three Egyptian Inspectors of the Department of Antiquities; the Representative of the Government Press Bureau; and all of Carter's colleagues and assistants.

The antechamber had been thoroughly swept by the gaffir and his men in the morning, who then placed chairs in a row, while the lights were focused on the wall betwixt the two tall statues.

Both Carter and Carnarvon were nervous, but for two very differing reasons.

That morning, in the Winter Palace Hotel, Mervyn Herbert, who had previously been told by Lord Carnarvon that he could not be present on this particular day, had wandered into his brother's room to say his customary 'Good morning'. He recorded the incident in his diary.

> This 'ceremony' was to be exceedingly private; nothing but officials and workers, so I understood. However, on Friday morning I went to Porch's room, as usual, before going out, to say 'Good morning'. He asked if I was free and said he would very much like me to go over with him to the Opening and support him, if he wanted it, but added 'I'm afraid I shall not be able to show you anything.' In any case I was delighted to go and, as we started at once, I only had time to send Elizabeth a message. If she had been dressed no doubt she would have come too. It was very bad luck and disappointing for her and I was terribly sorry she couldn't see this exciting ceremony. But there was nothing to be done about it.
>
> Porch and Evelyn and I started in his Ford and, after we had been going a few minutes, he said that it would really be all right and he could quite well get me in while the tomb was being opened. Then he whispered something to Evelyn and told her to tell me.
>
> This she did, under the strictest promise of secrecy – this is a thing I would never give away, in any case, and it is one which I think ought not to be known, at any rate, *for the present*.* Here is the secret. They had both already been into the second chamber! After the discovery they had not been able to resist it – they had made a small hole in the wall (which afterwards they filled up again) and afterwards climbed through. She described to me very shortly some of the extraordinary wonders I was about to see.

* Italics in original.

It was a most exciting drive. I cannot remember anything like it. The only others who know anything about it are the workmen; none of whom would ever breathe a word to a soul.

Pressmen, photographers, hundreds of tourists and at least one unofficial Egyptologist and author crowded three deep round the parapet wall. The sun was warm and the valley still.

It is said that a peasant made a prophecy upon this morning: 'These people are looking for gold, but they will find death.' One man, at least, on the parapet watched the proceedings with an objective eye. His status was not such that he could command an invitation as a guest – he was an author, but he knew his subject and remained outside.

As two o'clock drew near Lord Carnarvon, who appeared quite nervous, made an attempt at a jocular remark. His words just reached the onlookers.

'Right everyone, I think we are ready. We can now go down for our concert in the sepulchre!'

The writer was watching the proceedings from above and turned to a companion, giving a spontaneous reaction to the words he had heard. 'If he goes down in that spirit I give him six weeks to live.'

Gradually the tomb swallowed the V.I.P. party as they trooped down the passage, conscious of the historic revelation they were about to witness and bubbling with pent-up excitement. Gradually they took their seats on the chairs, while Carter and Carnarvon stood before them near the wall. Again Mervyn Herbert recorded his reactions, jotting them down in his diary.

Rows of chairs had been arranged in the first chamber of the tomb, which had been entirely cleared, except for the two statues of the king at one end. Between them was the sealed entrance and, at the bottom of this sealed door, was a little wooden platform which concealed the hole made in the wall when they (Lord Carnarvon and Lady Evelyn) had got in before. Porch, poor old fellow, was nervous, like a naughty schoolboy, fearing that they would discover that a hole had already been made. He was, alas – and most naturally – very excited; although he knew a good deal about what was there he cannot have helped feeling that this was one of the very great moments that happen to few people. He began by making a very fine little speech to all of us – short and to the point – one of the main things being thanks to all the workers, but principally to the Americans, who had very generously given their services free. Then Carter made a little speech – not very good – he was nervous – almost inarticulate, and talked mainly about science and the immensity of the discovery.

Now Carter took up a crowbar and, amidst a great hush of expectancy, thrust it at the top right-hand corner of the wall. It was a substantial edifice and when, eventually, he levered the first rock free he passed it down to Callender, who then placed it in a basket. Almost unnoticed by the onlookers a line of Egyptian workmen had descended behind the official party and now stood, silently waiting, a human chain ready to start passing back the baskets of rubble.

As the sound of the crowbar and chisel began to vibrate up to the entrance, the writer, on the parapet wall, happened to glance up at the sky. He saw a hawk, in ancient days the emblem of the Royal House, come swiftly over the hills from the direction of Thebes and hover just above their heads at the mouth of the tomb. It remained poised for a few moments, as if in mute witness of the scene, and then sailed away down the valley and into the west.

Carter managed to chip out the plaster surrounding the wooden lintel high above the door. He resisted the temptation to look through the small gap that was gradually appearing. After a full ten minutes he paused, picked up a torch and inserted it into the hole. The sight that met his eyes was breathtaking. It seemed that he was facing a solid wall of gold.

Renewing his efforts with mallet and chisel, hardly able to

control his excitement, he struggled to widen the hole, passing the rubble to Mace and Callender. In fact, he had to reduce the tempo of his work, chiselling with great care, for it seemed that the vast stretch of gold was only a few feet from his face. As a precaution he inserted a mattress, which he suspended from the lintel in order that nothing should fall within.

Unable to contain his curiosity any longer he picked up the torch and inserted it again. This was his moment of triumph, the culmination of twenty years' work, the sweet realisation of a lifetime's dream. Howard Carter was looking at the Burial Chamber of his long-sought King. His left arm dropped limply by his side and he could only stand immobile, lost in stupefied admiration. Difficult as it was to gain a general perspective the Sepulchral Chamber seemed to measure something like twenty feet by thirteen. The floor level was almost three feet below that of the antechamber, giving a ceiling height of ten feet or so. But the incredible fact was that all this area was taken up by a vast golden tabernacle, or shrine, which undoubtedly covered and guarded the sarcophagus of the king.

The structure was made of wood, covered in gold leaf, inlaid with beautiful blue-green porcelain, set between gilded symbols, which formed the decoration. Along its side a gilt winged serpent coiled away into the darkness. Beneath was a broad golden band on which an inscription read: 'All the gods who are in the Underworld declare that the King, the Lord of the Two Lands of Egypt, Lord of the Creations of the Sun of Ra, who loves him, Tutankhamen . . .'

Lower down two magical eyes were engraved on the side of the shrine. Through them the dead pharaoh could behold all that was happening. Perhaps, even now, the jackal-headed Anubis was carrying the king's soul to the Judgement Hall of Osiris, there to weigh his heart in the balances against the symbol of Truth, trusting that the king would not be found wanting.

Around the shrine, resting upon the ground, were the many funerary emblems, including the seven magic oars that Tutank hamen would need to propel him across the dark waters of the underworld.

It had taken almost two hours to demolish the wall and, when the task was complete, Lord Carnarvon and M. Lacau stepped into the chamber behind Carter, who took with him a long-lead light. Slowly, without a word being spoken and whilst the audience behind tried hard to contain their excitement, the three men deftly circumnavigated the shrine. Two beautiful alabaster vases blocked their way and, marking their position, Carter moved them for safety. The overall size of the shrine was so enormous (seventeen feet by eleven, and nine feet high) that it dwarfed the archaeologists. Each side of it was wrought with magic symbols which should ensure its safety and strength.

At the eastern end stood two great folding doors, closed and bolted.

Now, at the highest pitch of his nervous tension, Carter held before him the electric light. The bolts were not sealed and there was no knowing if the tomb robbers had been there before him. With hands that he found were unexpectedly trembling he took secure hold of the bolt, the first man to do so for three millennia. He exerted a steady pressure and, fantastically, the lock slid smoothly back. Moving himself forward, in order to make space for the door, Carter slowly eased it open. Hardly daring to look he riveted his eyes on the seal. In a moment of wild exaltation he let out a cry. The seals of the pharaoh were intact. All that lay before them, whatever it might be, had been untrammelled by human hand, unseen by any eye since one day in March or April three thousand two hundred and sixty-five years before, the young and mysterious king had been laid to his eternal rest.

CHAPTER SEVEN

DEATH ON SWIFT WINGS

LORD CARNARVON gazed in awe and wonderment at the
contents of the Sepulchral Chamber. Above the inner shrine
was draped a diaphanous, linen pall, decorated with delicate
golden rosettes. It had about it an ethereal solemnity as if, in
its very fragility, it besought no one to touch it.

As they walked round the shrine, stepping carefully over the
oars and other objects placed in meticulous position by the
departing priests, they came upon yet another low entrance to
a chamber, smaller than those so far found and by no means
so lofty. This doorway had not been sealed and, falling to their
knees, both Carnarvon and Carter, patron and mentor, respectively directed their gaze within. A single glance was sufficient
to tell them that this small room held such a store of exquisite
artefacts that this, indeed, must be the treasure chamber.

Within it, immediately facing them, was a shrine-shaped
chest overlaid with gold and surmounted by a cornice of cobras.
Surrounding it were four statues, tutelary goddesses of the dead
with outstretched, protective arms, seeking, with eyes of com-
passion, protection for their long-dead master. It was so impressive, the quintessence of simplicity, that Carter felt a lump in
his throat. Without doubt it was the Canopic Chest in which
was stored the human vitals of the pharaoh, that is with the
exception of his heart.

Then they saw the jackal god, Anubis, crouching within his
shrine and, behind him, the head of a sacred bull.

In the centre was a row of magnificent caskets of ivory and

Demolishing the wall (the seals clearly to be seen) between the antechamber and the burial chamber. Howard Carter with a crow-bar in his hand.

wood, decorated and inlaid with gold and blue faience. One of these was open and it contained an exquisite ostrich-feather fan, with ivory handle. Its state of preservation was perfect.

Reluctantly the principals gave way to their guests who, one by one, entered the chamber until, over an hour later, they filed out from the bowels of the earth, bemused and lost in contemplation.

For the onlookers surrounding the parapet the sombre procession presented a very strange sight. No sign of excitement or happiness, no laughter or tasteless triumph; just simple humility. More than anyone, Adamson noted, Lord Carnarvon seemed the most affected. It would be one of the last occasions that the military policeman would see him alive.

As ever, he was considerate and courteous to his guests, but said very little, and, gradually, as they partook of their buffet, the spirits of the archaeologists were restored by the warm glow of the sun and the wine that they drank from goblets. Gradually their wonderment gave way to animated conversation, as each queried with the other the details of those objects they had seen.

An hour later, as deep shadows began to grope their way across the chasm, Carter singled out Adamson and told him that the guests would be going down to his house, Castle Carter, as he always called his house. 'Now, Richard, as usual I am depending on you for security. Don't forget to lock the gates behind you.'

A few hours later, when all was quiet, Adamson took down his bed and set it up in its usual place in the antechamber. He bolted and padlocked the steel door behind him, then picked up one of the long, lead lights. In curiosity he noticed that one of the bulbs had been taken. Switching it on he examined the Sepulchral Chamber. He was astonished at the size of the shrine and the complexity of the decoration upon it.

He had heard of the magical rites enacted by the priests who required spiritual guardians to protect the sleep of the pharaoh. The method they employed was to select certain key slaves and torture them, almost to the point of death. While yet still conscious the sorcerer would instruct the victim, by way of hypnotic command, to guard the king with his spirit and pursue to destruction anyone that desecrated or disturbed the peace of the tomb. The slaves were then put to death while the instruction was still at the forefront of their minds.

Adamson had not been the slightest impressed. He was not superstitious and the dead were just dead, so far as he was concerned. If not, their spirits would have haunted the slopes of Passchendaele; but he had never seen a ghost. He marvelled at the workmanship of the shrine and little did he know, as he sat down upon his bed, that shortly he would go to sleep a mere few feet from a man-sized coffin, wrought throughout in solid gold.

Before doing so, however, he had to perform his daily chore of typing out Howard Carter's notes.

Lord Carnarvon, Lady Evelyn and the Honourable Mervyn Herbert returned to Luxor, where the latter sat down to write his diary.

It was very hot and stuffy in the tomb and, in spite of the thrilling excitement of it all, we were most of us glad to get into the air again. But I only heard one person who didn't enjoy it – a coon who was heard to say as he came out, 'that it had been a rotten, uncomfortable day and he couldn't think why he had been such a fool as ever to leave his club in Cairo!'

Porch and Evelyn and I stopped for tea at Carter's house. Although I had seen it almost every day I hadn't been inside since Christmas 1915, when he lent it to me. It was just the same. Callender and one or two of the other workers were staying there. We had a good and much needed tea and then drove back to Luxor.

The following night Mervyn Herbert continued with a description of the events of the second day.

The Sunday Opening, although nominally small, was naturally a much bigger occasion. The pressmen were hanging like vultures over the mouth of the tomb and there were a good many visitors – the queen of the Belgians – the Allenbys and a good many others. I took all our party, not knowing whom it might be possible to get in. Thank goodness all got in and saw the marvels and all were delighted. I felt rather ashamed of myself – I had not meant to try and see it again, when so many people were anxious to do so and when doing so gave a lot of trouble. But John said you must and seized Carter, which I had been unwilling to do, so I had one more sight of it, a very great treat indeed.

Porch, I think, had a very worrying time at Luxor, not that

he disliked it all; some of it amused him quite a lot. B U T the journalists were beyond belief. The prince of swine was, of course, W——, who is only satisfactory in one way; he looks as complete a cad as he is. In the hotel, where we all stayed, there were two groups of journalists – the sheep and the goats. The principal of the sheep was physically rather like one. W. and the rest were unutterable – they spied and lied and calumniated as I have not seen it done.

Porch showed me a letter from W. saying that he had been asked to do 'reporter' on the tomb. He didn't much like the job, but he put himself entirely in Porch's hands. He would do whatever he liked. Porch told him about the agreement he had made with *The Times* and why he had been obliged to do so. The next thing was W.'s series of venomous lies about Porch, about his having turned the whole thing into a commercial enterprise and so on. Some day I hope that man will get a bad time.

I had two days' fever, which kept me in bed. I don't know what it was, a sort of Egyptian chill, I suppose. Porch fed me on Brands' essence and novels, very successfully. The last I saw of the old fellow (Carnarvon) was in the hall of the Winter Palace Hotel, talking to Maxwell, Merton, *The Times* correspondent and others. I had said 'Good-bye' more than once. Maxwell had said to me that Porch ought to go to Aswan, as he needed a rest. I agreed that he was tired, although I don't think more so than was reasonably to be expected. Poor old fellow!

Lord Carnarvon was not destined to visit Aswan, the Cataracts, or Elephant Island. A few days later, as he walked out of the tomb, he was stung by a mosquito. This in itself was nothing, a mere irritation, if to be considered at all. However, the following morning, when he was shaving with his cut-throat razor, the blade nicked the top of the spot.

It cannot be disputed that he was tired and a little run-down. The following day he had a temperature and an angry reaction set in around the bite. His daughter put him to bed. Two days later he was up again and apparently recovered. He visited the site; then suddenly he had a relapse.

Lady Evelyn was nursing him personally and felt very concerned. She decided that he should be moved to Cairo immediately. They took the White Train, with Carnarvon wrapped up in blankets. Rooms were booked in the Continental Hotel. Within a very short time matters began to look more serious. Cables were exchanged between Cairo and England. Eventually Lady Evelyn suggested that her mother should quickly come out and bring with her Carnarvon's physician, Dr Johnson, an Australian. Howard Carter became extremely concerned for his friend and awaited each day's news with increasing anxiety.

A heavy mood of depression descended upon the excavators and newspapers reported Carnarvon's illness in detail. Inevitably rumours began to germinate.

It was a warm, still afternoon at the Wheeler Polo Ground, Meerut, in the United Province of India. The heat of the day had passed and now the balmy air carried the sweet scent of herbs and flowers to the several hundred onlookers who were enjoying the final clash betwixt the Seventh and Eleventh Hussars. The polo ground was good, flat and well made with excellent turf that suited this needle match to perfection.

On a raised and canopied dais the Viceroy, Lord Reading, and his guests, including Lord Inchcape, Chairman of the P. & O. Line, were enjoying the thrills of a close-run game. It was almost 4.30 p.m.; the teams were level and they were playing the very last chukka. The Seventh Hussars were captained by Herbert Fielden, and a subaltern, Lord Porchester, eldest son of Lord Carnarvon, was playing number two. In the last few seconds, with his polo stick almost entangled, a brief opportunity occurred and, with a push rather than a stroke, Porchester sent the ball spinning toward the goal. It hit the wicker of the goalpost, seemed to hesitate for a fraction, then, more by luck than intentional direction, spun round and over the line.

To the sound of tumultuous applause the teams, hot and weary, presented themselves to the Viceroy of India. The captain received the cup and each member a commemorative cup. It was just after he had shaken hands with His Excellency that a tall chuprassi of the Viceroy's Bodyguard diffidently stepped forward. He was a handsome Sikh, dressed in white, beturbaned and wearing the scarlet Viceregal sash. He addressed himself to Lord Porchester, bowing slightly as he did so.

'Sahib, a priority telegram from Egypt.'

He bowed again and retreated. Porchester took it in some surprise, glanced at the Viceroy and murmured: 'I wonder, Sir, if you would excuse me?'

'Of course, dear boy, I feel it must be further news of your dear father and his wonderful discovery.'

Still bathed in perspiration Henry Porchester slipped a finger behind the flap and tore the envelope open. He read the following:

FROM SIR JOHN MAXWELL, COMMANDER-IN-CHIEF, EGYPT, TO SIR CHARLES MUNROE, C.-IN-C. INDIA. URGENT. WILL YOU PLEASE EXPEDITE AN IMMEDIATE PASSAGE FOR LORD PORCHESTER TO THE CONTINENTAL HOTEL CAIRO WHERE HIS FATHER LORD CARNARVON IS VERY SERIOUSLY ILL.

Typed beneath the message, which had been redirected from his regimental H.Q. were the words: 'three months compassionate leave granted.' Suddenly the match was forgotten and a sympathetic silence descended on the Viceroy's party.

Lord Reading murmured: 'Oh, my dear boy, I am so sorry to hear this bad news.'

At which moment Lord Inchcape, standing at his side, also offered his condolences and then made a suggestion.

'Look here, Porchester, the *Narkunda* sails tomorrow and will be calling at Suez. I know she's full to the gunnels but I will instruct her captain to make available a junior officer's cabin. I shall also tell him to make maximum speed, the expenses of which . . .' he murmured as an aside, 'I shall naturally defray, in order that you can get to your father's bedside as soon as is humanly possible.'

Then it was the turn of Lord Reading: 'I also have a suggestion.'

He turned to one of his A.D.C.s, 'I've an idea we ought to put Porchester on my train and send him down to Bombay tonight; he will then have sufficient time in the morning without any fear of missing the sailing.'

'Yes, sir,' the A.D.C. agreed, 'a good idea.'

But suddenly he added, with deference: 'Perhaps I could suggest that instead we couple your personal coach to the Punjab Express. It'll reach Bombay by seven in the morning and Lord Porchester will enjoy a restful night and breakfast before his arrival. It will leave him ample time to reach the *Narkunda*.'

'Excellent.' The Viceroy smiled.

'You are too kind, sir,' Lord Porchester managed to stammer. 'I really don't know how to thank you.'

'Nonsense, my dear boy, we are all terribly concerned about your father.'

With barely sufficient time to make the necessary arrangements Lord Porchester returned to his quarters and earnestly discussed the situation with his wife. He had an intuitive feeling that he would not be returning to India. A telegram couched in such phrases seemed to indicate an illness of severe proportion; besides which his father, since his motor-car accident, was a very frail man.

Many turbulent emotions passed through his mind. It was all so totally unexpected. He felt deeply worried, but also had to admit to a tinge of excitement. With honesty he would recognise that he did not know his father very well. Through the vagaries of his traditional upbringing, coupled with many years spent at boarding school, followed immediately by his joining the army, he had never had an opportunity of knowing his parent in adulthood. This was a shame, for no one knew better than his son the accomplishments and talents of his father. His sister, Evelyn, had benefited greatly from being at home. Now it looked as if he might be embarking upon a solemn journey of farewell. Leaving his wife behind to pack and close their home Porchester boarded the *Narkunda*.

Steaming at some twenty to twenty-two knots they reached Aden, where the Chairman of the P. & O. had arranged double coolie lines to speed re-coaling. At Suez a launch came alongside with Sir John Maxwell's A.D.C. Expressing his very considerable thanks to the captain, Lord Porchester climbed down the companionway and was soon streaking across the harbour to the railway siding, at which stood Sir Charles Munroe's private train.

By two o'clock that afternoon he reached the Continental Hotel in Cairo. It was with very mixed emotions that, at the end of his long journey, Lord Porchester asked in reception for his father's suite. He felt an overwhelming sense of relief that he had arrived in time. Yet, as he waited to ascend in the lift, he could not help contemplating on the irony of fate that would seem to be denying his father the final satisfaction of completing his work on the discovery of the tomb.

As he stepped into the lift cage Porchester suddenly realised that it was over a year since he had last seen his parents, on the occasion of his wedding. But even that had been a mere interlude, for it was on Christmas Day 1916, that he had left Tilbury to sail in convoy round the Cape, before beginning his long period of service abroad. He remembered so well asking his father to take care of his little fox terrier bitch, Susie. The two had become devoted and he was saddened when Lord Carnarvon had written to tell him of the accident which had resulted in the amputation of her limb.

If there was one consolation in this situation it was the prospect of a family reunion, for the manager downstairs had explained that Lord Porchester's mother, together with her husband's Australian physician, had flown in a tiny Puss Moth right across Europe and over the Mediterranean, and were now in the hotel.

Porchester was ushered into the outer room of the suite where two night nurses awaited him. Having introduced himself he asked after the patient.

'He's delirious at the moment, I'm afraid, sir.'

'Please, may I see him?'

'Of course. Actually, your mother said that she would like to take you in herself, but at the moment she's sleeping. I'm afraid she's very tired.'

'Oh, we must not disturb her. I'll go in alone,' Porchester quickly instructed. Treading softly he followed the nurses into the bedroom.

There lay his father, unshaven, with bloodshot eyes and yellow foam flecking his lips; a pulse in his throat seemed to twitch in irregular spasms. It was quite obvious that he was desperately ill. Lord Carnarvon's son stepped forward and took his father's hand. It was over-hot and seemed somewhat lifeless.

'Papa, this is your son, Henry. I've come all the way from India to see you.'

His father turned his head and stared at him. His reaction was extraordinary.

'Do you remember how those Italians ran like rabbits on the PiarVi?' Porchester returned his father's gaze in astonishment. Lord Carnarvon had never been in the army, had never worn uniform, being far too frail in health, but yet this was his reaction to the arrival of his son.

For a second or two Porchester was so nonplussed that he could find no words to make reply, then he managed to stammer: 'Oh, yes papa dear, they did, they did.'

His lordship continued: 'We ought to have shelled them and shot them like rabbits . . .'

Obviously required to say something in response to this feverish outburst Lord Porchester could only exclaim: 'Ha! Ha! Yes, I am sure you are right.'

Whereupon he turned round and caught the eye of one of

A visit by the Duke and Duchess of Connaught to the Valley of the Kings when Howard Carter was still searching. The desolation of the Valley of the Dead is self evident from this early photograph.

the nurses, whose expression seemed to indicate, 'take no notice, he is completely delirious.'

As Lord Carnarvon's son looked down upon his father he was almost overwhelmed by his deep sense of sadness. Here he was,

E

all the way from India, standing obediently at his father's bedside, totally unrecognised.

What an extraordinary man his father had been. Frail in
health, yet an adventurer who had travelled the world; a great
collector of antiques; a man interested in the occult and spiritualism; a politician and businessman; an artist in photography,
and an extraordinary breeder of the racehorse. Finally, he had
added archaeology to his long list of talents. Desperately untidy,
often unpredictable, yet urbane and generous to a degree, he
now, indisputably, lay dying.

Feeling suddenly weary and very low in spirit, Lord Porchester quietly left the room, asking the nurses to call him
should anything occur.

Later in the day he was sadly re-united with his family.

That night he retired early to his bedroom, placed his torch
beside his bed, undressed and fell into fitful slumber. It seemed
that his head had no sooner touched the pillow than he was
conscious of an insistent knocking on the door.

Suddenly he was awake, glanced at his watch, which read
five to two, and called 'Come in.' It was one of the nurses.

'Lord Porchester, hurry, hurry. I am afraid your father has
passed away; your mother has just shut his eyes. She would
like you to go in and say a little prayer while his hands are still
warm.'

For a moment he sat immobile as the words sank in, and then
he could only murmur: 'Oh dear; of course I'll come right
away.'

Quickly snatching his dressing-gown and running a comb
through his hair, Porchester picked up his pocket torch and
went out into the corridor. Even as he was walking to his
father's suite the lights in the passage suddenly went out and
the hotel was plunged into darkness.

Hesitating for only a second to find the switch on his torch
he continued to walk rapidly to his father's bedroom. Inside he
found his mother, crying quietly on her knees. He quickly joined
her. After a few minutes with his arm around her shoulder he

decided that she should be left alone, and quietly tiptoed from the room. He found it hard to contain his emotions.

Suddenly the lights went on again, some five minutes or so after the failure. In the room outside people were already gathering and Lord Porchester found his sister, Evelyn, terribly upset, as were all members of the family and their friends, who included Howard Carter.

Dr Johnson went into the bedroom and came out again shortly. Eventually Lady Almina joined them and, for half an hour, the family engaged in desultory conversation. It was then suggested that probably the wisest move would be for everyone to return to bed.

The following morning Lord Porchester awoke to the full realisation of the family's loss and the effect it would have upon all their lives. He dressed slowly and pensively and then went down to the dining-room for breakfast. There he found Howard Carter, whom he hardly knew. He sat at his table. One glance was sufficient to inform him that Carter felt the loss just as much as any member of the family, for the two men had lived and worked together for many, many years and Carnarvon, in addition, had been his generous benefactor.

He immediately explained to Lord Porchester exactly what had happened: 'Your father had a little mosquito bite, which he nicked with his razor, but it seemed to have no significance at all. He put some iodine and cotton wool on it and thought no more. That evening he told your sister that he felt he might have a chill coming on. When Lady Evelyn took his temperature it was reading a hundred and one but, strangely enough, by the morning it had returned to normal – if anything, slightly sub-normal. She kept him in bed for two days. Your father then felt quite well enough to come out to the dig but that evening seemed to take a turn for the worse and, when your sister found that his temperature had risen to a hundred and one again, she decided forthwith to take him to Cairo. It was the best thing she could have done. He was apparently quite comfortable and received all the medical attention available. It was obvious that he had contracted some sort of poisoning, but after ten days the worst seemed over, so much so that he was able to sit up for a few hours in the day. I am afraid that must have caused his final relapse for, during the night, he became seriously ill and his physicians diagnosed virus pneumonia.'

Porchester ordered his breakfast and noticed that Carter was glancing at the three Cairo newspapers. He murmured: 'You notice that the news of your father's death has been recognised by a black mourning band round all the papers. He was very well loved here in Egypt; more so, of course, since we found the tomb.'

The newspapers were printed in Arabic and Carter began to read. Suddenly Porchester noticed him stiffen with apparent irritation. Next he was clucking his tongue and exclaimed 'how preposterous!'

Porchester looked up: 'What's the matter?'

'Oh, these people. I don't know if you were aware of it, but last night there was an electricity failure . . .'

'As a matter of fact, I was,' Lord Porchester cut in, 'because I was walking down the corridor to my father's room at the time.'

'Well, the newspapers have concocted a story that the lights were put out by the express command of King Tut. They say, in effect, that your father, an infidel, had ignored all the warnings and disturbed the sacred remains of King Tutankhamen. To uphold his sovereignty the king has taken his vengeance and, in order that all should mark his displeasure, he turned out every single light in the city of Cairo at the moment your father passed away.'

Lord Porchester was not much in the mood for frivolity and merely grunted. It was at this moment that a message was handed him at the table. It was a request from Lord Allenby that he should very kindly present himself at the Residency at ten o'clock.

Five minutes before the appointed time the young subaltern arrived for his interview with the field-marshal. He was not kept waiting, immediately being ushered into a salon. Lord Porchester brought his heels together and bowed to the regal figure that stood before him. He also noticed that another man of military bearing, but in civilian clothes, was standing beside him. 'My dear Porchester, how very good of you to come. I really am most terribly sorry about the passing of your father. This must have been a terrible blow. I'm only so grateful that you managed to reach Cairo in time.'

'You're too kind, sir.'

The field-marshal cleared his throat: 'I asked you to come over because I felt we owed you some explanation for the story that has appeared in the press. I have to admit that it's quite extraordinary. Firstly, may I introduce you to Colonel Cornwall, who is head of the Cairo Electricity Board.'

The two men shook hands.

'I don't know if you read this morning's papers, but it gives some prominence to the failure of the electricity supply during the night.'

Lord Allenby turned to the colonel. 'Cornwall, perhaps you would explain to Lord Porchester, in your own words, exactly what occurred.'

'Certainly, sir. I was in bed at the time and was suddenly awakened by a telephone call from my senior duty manager. He told me that there had been a major power failure throughout the city, but that he had been unable to locate the cause. I noted the time, which was 2 a.m. Would I please come immediately. Naturally I agreed to do so, dressed and had just got out my car when, to my surprise, all the street lights went on again. However, having got so far, I thought I might as well continue. When I arrived it was to find that all my officials were completely baffled. There seemed no reason for the failure whatsoever. The breakers were in position, the fuses intact.'

He paused for a moment.

'As you may or may not know, Lord Porchester, the city is divided into four separate areas and, therefore, I decided to visit each of the other districts to hear what they had to say. In every case the story was the same. For something just over five minutes the lights went out and then went on again. I am afraid there is no technical explanation whatsoever.'

The first task confronting Lord Porchester was to arrange for his father to be embalmed, prior to taking him home to High-clere Castle. Howard Carter was also anxious that Porchester should visit the tomb and this he agreed to do directly a suitable booking had been made on a ship. This turned out to be far more difficult than he had envisaged. Mariners are a super-stitious crowd and most sea captains will do everything possible to avoid taking a coffin on board. In due course he succeeded. He then visited Luxor and returned to find that his wife had just reached Cairo. Now they could embark for England.

It was a sad and subdued voyage which ended when Lord Carnarvon was 'laid in state' in the tiny chapel of Highclere Castle. He had expressed the wish to be buried in a coffin of Highclere oak on Beacon Hill, overlooking his home, and his son selected the site as requested by his father. Carnarvon also required that neither headstone nor tomb should mark the place of his burial.

After Lord Carnarvon had been laid to rest, overlooking his stud farm and the window of his bedroom, the new sixth earl received a telephone call. It was a lady on the other end of the line: 'Is that Lord Carnarvon?' she inquired.

'It is,' he replied.

'Oh, I am so glad. You won't know me at all, but I am a spiritualist and worked very closely with your father. In fact, at our seances, I acted as his medium.'

The new incumbent of the title was somewhat taken aback, but managed to make a polite reply by saying: 'Oh, how interesting.'

The lady continued: 'But, far more important than that, I have to tell you that I had a message from your father two days ago.'

'Really!' Lord Carnarvon murmured, just slightly put out.

'Yes, we had a very long conversation and he has asked me to pass on an instruction to you. It is that on no account whatsoever should you ever step inside the tomb of King Tutankhamen again. Under no circumstances,' she repeated with emphasis. 'This is the express wish of your late father and he asked me to tell you. He pointed out that if you disobey his order you will surely die and this would mean an end to the House of Herbert for, as yet, I understand,' she said, 'you have no children.'

Lord Carnarvon thanked the lady for her trouble and told her that he would be happy to carry out his father's wish.

Looking back and trying to analyse his reaction, he came to the opinion that he had agreed for a number of reasons. First, that he did not wish to offend the lady; the second that, if indeed this was the wish of his father, he would be the last person in the world to demur. Thirdly, he had found the tomb somewhat uninteresting and could see no reason why he should ever wish to return. Lastly, he had, in fact, attended two seances with his father at Highclere Castle, which the late earl used to conduct in the East Anglia bedroom.

He had watched Lady Cunliffe Owen put into a trance on an occasion when Howard Carter had also been present. It had been an eerie, not to say, unpleasant experience which had shaken the young man quite considerably. One moment the lady had been her normal self, the next her features had become strained and white. Suddenly she had started talking in an unknown tongue which, to everyone's astonishment, Howard Carter had pronounced as being Coptic. On another occasion he had personally seen flowers levitate from a bowl, and he remembered one seance when Lady Evelyn had been placed in a trance. It was for this reason that Lord Carnarvon, however sceptical he might be, would not dismiss the matter out of hand. However, he would far prefer not to concern himself with these beliefs personally.

Some weeks later he received one further telephone call – the last of its kind.

'Lord Carnarvon, I hate to disturb you, but your father came through again last night. He asked me if I had passed on his message and whether you had acquiesced. I answered both questions in the affirmative. He said how pleased he was; that he sent his love and was glad that everything was now going so well for you.'*

* These were the only two contacts the present Lord Carnarvon ever had in regard to this matter.

CHAPTER EIGHT

PRELUDE TO TRIUMPH

IN Luxor a saddened Howard Carter, who had not attended the family funeral, returned to the scene of the discovery. The heat in the Valley of the Kings was now building up to its summer intensity. Within the tomb itself the temperature could rise from anything between ninety-five and a hundred and ten degrees. Activity underground would now have to stop until the autumn. Accordingly Carter gave instructions for the tomb to be resealed.

Work in the laboratories, under Mace and Callender, proceeded apace. Having carried out innumerable and complex preservation techniques the objects had been wrapped in cotton wool and linen, prior to being packed in eighty-nine boxes. These boxes, in turn, had been transferred to thirty-four stout packing cases for their trip down the Nile to the Cairo Museum.

As might be expected the weights involved were considerable and the problem arose as to how to manhandle this freight to the bank of the Nile, some four and a half miles away.

It was decided that the burden would be too great for camels and that human porterage would be both arduous and risky. The solution found was the use of the Décauville railway. This ingenious method comprised portable sections of rail bolted to light wooden sleepers that could be fitted together, to give an overall length of one hundred yards or so. The trucks would be loaded with the packing cases and then, with the help of fifty labourers, the train would be pushed to the limit of the rail, which would then be taken up from behind and relaid in front

The Royal Kas – the
abode of the
Pharaoh's soul. They
had performed their
sentinel duty for
over three thousand
years. To Howard
Carter they became
persons and he
talked to them.

Photo: Griffith Institute

again. Thus, by a series of leap-frogging manœuvres, the invaluable cargo was steadily manhandled down toward the bank of the river. This not inconsiderable task was completed in fifteen working hours, spread over two days. Upon arrival at the Nile it was found that the water was too low to allow the barges to come close in shore; thus the last few yards were accomplished on the shoulders of the workmen, who hoisted the packing cases on board from the sandy shallows. The worst part of the journey was thus accomplished safely.

The fact that the tomb had been sealed and the first consignment of treasures despatched in no way seemed to lessen the public interest in the excavators' activities, which now, to all intents and purposes, had virtually ceased for the summer. To

whet the appetite of the watching world, journalists began their task by following up the death of Lord Carnarvon with highly lurid reports of the curse on the tomb. Of the many inscriptions found on objects in the tomb and especially on the Golden Shrine, none bore the now famous words: 'Death shall come on swift wings to him who disturbs the sleep of the pharaoh.'

Similar injunctions that gave ease of adaptability had been found on the tombs of lesser nobles in the Necropolis of Thebes. One such, written upon a mortuary-statue of a certain Ursu, a mining engineer who lived less than a hundred years before the time of Tutankhamen, states: 'He who trespasses upon my property, or who shall injure my tomb, or drag out my mummy, the Sun-god shall punish him. He shall not bequeath his goods to his children; his heart shall not have pleasure in life; he shall not receive water (for his spirit to drink) in the tomb; and his soul shall be destroyed forever.'

Another inscription in Aswan reads: 'As for any man who shall enter into this tomb . . . I will pounce upon him as on a bird; he shall be judged for it by the great god.'

At this time the Honourable Richard Bethell, son of Lord Westbury, was acting as Carter's secretary and general factotum. The archaeologist was again besieged by the press and nothing was calculated to rouse their interest more than discussion of 'the curse of the pharaohs'.

Howard Carter became incensed with what he considered to be preposterous supposition and recorded his thoughts thus.

It has been stated in various quarters that there are actual physical dangers hidden in Tutankhamen's tomb – mysterious forces, called into being by some malefic power, to take vengeance on whomsoever should dare to pass its portals. There was, perhaps, no place in the world freer from risks than the tomb. When it was opened, scientific research proved it to be sterile. Whatever foreign germs there may be within it today have been introduced from without . . .

However, even Howard Carter was not immune from mysterious circumstances. As has been stated, he owned a canary which lived in a cage in his bungalow amidst the sand and desolation, bringing pleasure and joy to Carter in his lonelier hours.

His house servants used to place the cage outside in order that the bird might enjoy an airing. On one occasion shortly after Lord Carnarvon's death it had been trilling to its heart's content when, suddenly, it fell silent. Carter's manservant, marking the cessation of song, rushed outside to see what had happened. He saw, swaying on its coils and standing erect, a jet black cobra in the very act of swallowing its prey. Somehow it had managed to infiltrate the wire bars, mesmerised the little bird and snatched it to its untimely death. The sacred cobra in Ancient Egypt was guardian of the king.

The news spread like wildfire, to such an effect that an important official of the Egyptian government brought to the valley the famous snake charmer, Mussa. This man visited the tomb – some considerable distance from Carter's bungalow – and drew from it both another cobra and a grass snake. How they arrived there no one knew, but certain it is that this incident added fuel to the fire of the current superstition. Howard Carter remained unmoved, if sad at the loss of his canary.

Another shadow began to throw its dark mantle over the excavators in the valley.

Upon the death of Lord Carnarvon his wife, the Countess Almina, and the executors to the estate, including the new earl, expressed their wish that Howard Carter should be allowed, under their patronage, to complete his long and arduous work in the tomb in spite of the realisation that this might well take many years to accomplish. Howard Carter and the family assumed that the basis of Lord Carnarvon's concession should automatically transfer 'to his heirs and assigns'. The Egyptian government argued to the contrary. They declared that the concession had been a personal one vested in his lordship and, that now he had passed away, all rights reverted to them. This, at the least, could be described as desperately unfair.

Lord Carnarvon had invested generously for over a decade and had received little or no financial recompense. The contemporary basis for a concession to explore and excavate was designed to assist both parties; the government, having no funds for archaeology, required the help of patrons. They, on their part, must expect some reward for their investment and labour. The problem was resolved by allowing the excavator to assume ownership of duplicate articles that he might find. These he was entitled to add to his own collection, or to sell to museums, usually in the country of his origin. There were, however, various safeguards in the national interest of Egypt, and three clauses in Lord Carnarvon's Concession covered such an eventuality.

(a) Mummies of a king, prince, high priest, or member of the court, together with the sarcophagus and coffin, shall be the property of the Department of Antiquities.

(b) Tombs which are discovered intact, as well as their contents, shall be the property of the museum.

(c) In the case of tombs not completely ransacked, the Department of Antiquities shall keep mummies, sarcophagi, and all objects of the first importance to history or archaeology, and divide the rest with the concession holder.

Considering that the tomb of Tutankhamen had, without doubt, been ransacked by tomb robbers, it seemed reasonable that the Carnarvon Estate should benefit under Clause (c). The Egyptian government, however, decided to claim the entire contents, under the proviso 'objects of the first importance'.

For their part the family and executors held that their first consideration must be the support of Howard Carter, who was solely dedicated to preserving the treasures for posterity and to record, with all scientific means possible, every last detail of the discovery. From this course the archaeologist would not be deflected. On the other hand, no one more than he appreciated the generosity of his benefactor and he, in turn, felt that it was only right and proper that the family should see some return, at least, for their financial outlay over the last ten years, if not some recompense for the decade of devoted work by Carnarvon.

For the moment there was an uneasy peace; with interminable exchanges of communication, a never-ending stream of tourists and the world's press, standing in the noonday sun. It did not auger well for the autumn. Much of the ill-will was occasioned, not unnaturally, by the climate of the contemporary political scene. The Egyptians were intent on throwing off the yoke of

British colonial rule and any incident likely to call into question their national rights and heritage was bound to cause friction.

One such tiny incident occurred in July. On the tenth of the month *The Times* published a long letter from Sir Martin Conway, M.P., which was headed: 'Monuments of Egypt; Failure of local custodians; Neglected Antiquities.' The second paragraph of his letter was not calculated to improve harmonious relations between the English excavators and the Cairo Museum.

> Taking the two great museums first, the policy of Egypt for the Egyptian means the replacement of Europeans by Egyptian employees in such vital functions, for example, as the repair and setting up for exhibition of ancient objects. The delicate treasures recovered from Tutankhamen's tomb, for instance, when brought to the museum, need to be handled only by the most experienced craftsmen. It may be asserted that, in all the museums of the world put together, there are not a dozen men skilful enough to be entrusted with such a responsibility and, among that dozen, certainly not one Egyptian or Oriental is to be numbered. Nevertheless, the demand is beginning to be made that all the European craftsmen employed by the museums shall be replaced by Egyptians. It is easy to prophesy what will be the fate of many a treasure when that revolution has been accomplished, and how a steady degradation of the whole collection is bound to follow.

King Fuad immediately acted in response to this criticism and ordered an official inquiry into the work and preservation of ancient monuments in Egypt. He allocated to this task the annual sum of twenty thousand Egyptian pounds. In addition, the king requested the reasons why the Committee of Conservation had not met since June 1922.

In the meantime, and after lengthy negotiations with the Department of Antiquities, Almina, countess of Carnarvon, was authorised to continue the excavation of Tutankhamen's tomb up to the period ending 1 November 1924.

At long last the heat of the summer gave way to the more equable climatic conditions of autumn and, on 8 October, Howard Carter returned to Egypt and Cairo preparatory to commencing the second season's work in the burial chamber. Expectation began to run high and enthusiasm gripped both the archaeologists and their Egyptian labour force. Yet again the rubble was removed from the stairway and Carter and his team made entry to the tomb, while Adamson prepared for his night-time vigils underground.

Reluctantly, Carter decided that the time had come to remove

One of the several 'opening' ceremonies. This one was attended by Lord and Lady Allenby. The food was sent across the Nile from the Winter Palace Hotel some four and a half miles away.

Photo: 'The Times'

the two guardian Kas, whose sentinel duty had fortunately exceeded the allotted three-thousand-year span. He had gazed at them so often, endeavouring to fathom their innermost thoughts, that now, with their absence, he would feel a personal loss. Carter frequently communed with them, but consideration for their safety was paramount and, now that the dividing wall between the antechamber and the burial chamber was about to be demolished, there was no alternative but to remove them.

Anyway the king's spirit should long since have been ushered into the Palace of the Gods by Ra himself, greeted by Isis, Nephthys and the Glorified Ones. At his judgement, having been found not wanting, he could take up his future abode in the north-eastern part of the sky, among the circumpolar stars. From here he would be invited by his majesty, Ra, to join his company and travel through the night sky in the boat called Mesketet, and through the dark sky in the boat called Manzet.

In order to protect the statues the carpenters erected great wooden frames with securing planks to keep them upright. Then Callender and Carter swathed them in bandages, preparatory to their removal to the laboratory. Here they would receive meticulous attention before being shipped on their inglorious passage to the modern capital and their ultimate home, the Cairo Museum.

Such choice of a final resting place for all eternity seemed somewhat out of sympathy with the impressive legend that they bore. 'The Good God of whom one be proud, the Sovereign of whom one boasts, the Royal Ka of Harakhte, Osiris, the King Lord of the Lands, Nebkheperure'.

Upon the safe removal of the Kas, Carter, Callender and Mace set about the demolition of the partition wall. It was constructed of dry masonry, reinforced with wooden logs, the whole plastered over. Work proceeded but slowly, great care being needed to prevent it from collapsing on to the shrine. Conditions were by no means ideal, with a general lack of air, considerable heat and vast quantities of dust.

In due course the last stone was removed and there before them stood the tabernacle. The walls of the burial chamber were coated with gypsum plaster, painted yellow, with a white dado all round. The ceiling was in its natural state, hewn to meticulous proportions, with ten thousand chisel marks maintaining a geometric perfection.

Upon the walls of the funerary chamber were painted many scenes depicting, at the eastern end, the funeral procession of the king. One part of it, at least, is unique, in that it depicts Tutankhamen's successor, King Ay, presiding over the funeral ceremony.

An ancient account of such a funeral, recorded on a stele approximately one hundred years before Tutankhamen, describes the ceremony in detail.

> A goodly burial arrives in peace, thy seventy days having been fulfilled in thy place of embalming. Thou art placed on the bier and art drawn by bulls without blemish, thy road being besprinkled with milk until thou reachest the door of thy tomb. The children of thy children, united of one accord, weep with loving hearts. Opened is thy mouth by the lector, and thy purification is made by the Sem priest. Horus adjusts for thee thy mouth and opens for thee thy eyes and ears, thy flesh and thy bones being perfect in all that appertains to thee. There are recited for thee spells and glorifications. There is made for thee an offering, which the king gives, thy own true heart being with thee . . . Thou comest in thy former shape, even as on the day wherein thou wast born. There is brought to thee the son thou lovest, the courtiers making obeisance. Thou enterest into the land given of the king, into the sepulchre of the west, there to be performed rites as for those of yore.

The scene on the wall of the burial chamber actually showed the mummy supported on a lion-shaped bier, within a shrine on a boat, which, in turn, rests upon a sledge. The dead king is festooned with garlands. On the prow of the boat is a sphinx. Nobles, priests and officials walk beside the bier, each person wearing upon his wig or shaven head a white linen filet. White pennants flutter at the bow and stern of the boat. A legend records:

> The Courtiers of the Royal Household going in procession with Osiris, King Tutankhamen to the west. They cry: 'Oh King! Come in peace! Oh God, Protector of the Land.'

The next task of the excavators was to photograph, preserve and then remove the hundreds of objects lying in ceremonial position on the floor of the sepulchre chamber. The workmanship of these articles was breathtaking. For instance, a simple, plain, gold stick with a lapis lazuli glass top, inscribed, 'Take for thyself the wand of gold in order that thou mayest follow thy beloved father, Amen, most beloved of gods.'

There was another stick, inlaid with glass and golden filigree, which was entitled, 'The beautiful stick of his majesty.' Beside these lay a plain reed, richly mounted, but unadorned compared with the others. The reason for its inclusion became obvious with the description, 'A reed which his majesty cut with his own hand.'

There were alabaster vases, a series of curved batons, most elaborately decorated, iridescent elytra of beetles and broad bands of burnished gold, with scroll-patterned borders. There were gold and silver sticks, ceremonial maces, staves and bows. Within the walls were niches facing north, south, east and west, in which stood magical figures, whose tasks were to vanquish the dark powers of the nether world and to repel the enemy of Osiris, in whatsoever form that he might come.

At long last the excavators were about to embark on the most dramatic stage of their discovery. Until now Carter's professionalism had refused all temptation to proceed until every single object had been catalogued, labelled, photographed, preserved and removed to safety. Now, and only now, was he prepared to break the seal on the second shrine. How many lesser men would have given way to their curiosity and cut those simple knots. But first they must unhinge the heavy dais of the outer shrine.

The joinery work of the Ancient Egyptian carpenters was supreme. Callender estimated that each section weighed anything up to half a ton, possibly more, and were sometimes joined

Photo: 'The Times'

The Queen of the Belgians and the Crown Prince, who travelled up to Luxor for the opening of the burial chamber.

together by wooden tongues, but often by solid bronze. If it had not been for the natural shrinkage of the wood after three thousand years, revealing the clues to its construction, this shrine itself might have defied the meticulous archaeologist determined to occasion it no harm.

Gradually, with patience, the joiners' secrets were revealed and fine saws cut through the tongues which, at least, enabled them to lift the roof. The headroom could be measured in inches but, as the shrine was constructed of two-and-a-quarter inch oak planking, overlaid with delicate gold work upon gesso, the use of hoists with differential gearing and leverage had to be employed.

Slowly, hour by hour, day by day, struggling and perspiring in the limited few feet of work room, they managed to dismantle the outer shrine. Their next problem was the linen pall, already much decayed and fragile with time, that completely enveloped the second shrine.

Dr Alexander Scott had experimented with a duroprene compound dissolved in an organic solvent, which strengthened the tissues to such an extent that they were able to roll it on to a great wooden roller. So far the undertaking had consumed eighty-four days of manual labour and the end of the year was at hand. But now, at last, Carter was ready to step back in time, even to before the tomb robbers, knowing full well that the last hand to shut and bolt the wooden doors was the high priest who had officiated at the funeral ceremony.

This day could never be repeated in a lifetime. Indeed, no one in the living world had yet experienced such a thrill.

Carter decided that, before he performed the act, the press should be granted one of their fortnightly visits to mark their progress. The date was 31 December 1923.

One of the many reports published in London read as follows.

> One and all seemed vastly impressed with the great size of the shrine, and the obvious difficulty which the dismantling presents. When they saw the roof sections leaning against the wall of the antechamber with, close by, the pole round which the pall was wrapped yesterday, they realised what a colossal task their removal must have constituted, and all seemed impressed with the extensive precautions taken to avoid damage to the shrine during the dismantling operations.

By now the entire world was hanging on every report from Luxor, and Howard Carter, with his entire staff, supplemented by the Chief Inspector of Antiquities, R. Engelbach, also Messrs Harkness, Lythgoe and Winlock, decided that the moment had come to open the door of the second shrine.

It was almost a match to the first, beautifully constructed in gilt and inlaid with blue faience. The doors were bolted at the top and bottom. Carter stepped forward, nervously glanced around him, smiled to his colleagues and, without more ado, cut the cord. With the greatest of care he removed the all-important seal whose intactness bore witness that no one had been there before him. It was made of clay and was imprinted with two distinct seals, the first embodying Tutankhamen's pre-nomen, 'Kheperu-neb-Re', and the second, the Royal Necropolis Seal, 'The Jackal over nine Foes'.

Crouching on his knees Carter drew back the door and, as the light flooded the interior, beheld yet a third shrine, perfect in condition, as beautiful, if not more so, than the first two. There was no point in holding back now. Again the doors were bolted and sealed. The archaeologist completed the same operation and gently opened the third set of doors.

By now the suspense was unbearable, probably even more so for the onlookers than for Carter himself. Again he drew back the doors and peered inside. This time, to his amazement, a fourth golden shrine confronted him, even more perfect, if that were possible, than the rest. But this time no seals barred his way. Without a pause Carter leaned forward and opened what he believed to be the last set of doors.

Sliding back the bolts he gently opened them, drawing in his breath as he did so, for there before his eyes stood a vast sarcophagus, handhewn from a huge, single piece of yellow quartzite. Sculptured into its corners were the figures and wings of four goddesses, guarding the final resting-place of the dead boy-king. It was eloquent, ethereal, appealing to all that was best in the instincts and emotions of man. With limpid tranquility the goddesses simply implored peace for their master.

Carter moved to one side, unable to speak, while his colleagues crowded round in silent admiration.

As Carter later described, 'it was a perfect Egyptian elegy in stone.'

It was some minutes before they began to appreciate the next problem that confronted them. Lying atop the sarcophagus was a vast piece of rose-pink granite, designed by its architects to defy any movement for all time. Its weight alone, notwithstanding that of the sarcophagus, was one and a quarter tons. How could they remove it and what lay within?

CHAPTER NINE

COFFINS OF A KING

THE readers of *The Times* were now enjoying a serial of epic grandeur.

The following day the headlines ran:

TUTANKHAMEN'S TOMB INTACT

A decisive stake was reached in the work at the tomb of Tutankhamen yesterday. Mr Howard Carter succeeded in opening the doors of the remaining three shrines and discovered a stone sarcophagus, colossal in size, magnificent in workmanship and, beyond any question, intact.

On 3 January they were told that Professor Newberry had spent the morning in the laboratory examining the funerary bouquets discovered in the sepulchre chamber. He found them to be composed of branches of persea and olive. The former tree, which is not indigenous to Egypt, was apparently introduced from Abyssinia and Somaliland where it was extensively grown under the New Empire. Like the olive the persea was regarded as a sacred tree, which explains why both were selected for the funerary bouquets.

On 7 January Carter gave a detailed interview.

Our work this season, confined to the sepulchre chamber and within the first doors of the great shrine, has been on wholly untouched ground. Though thieves had entered the antechamber, the so-called annexe, and the storechamber, and deranged the objects there while hunting for portable loot, here within the great shrine, as the original seals on the doors of the inner shrine indicate, no one has entered since the King was laid to rest.

Thus, through some great piece of good fortune, we at last found what we had been longing for, but never dreamed of obtaining – an absolute insight into the funerary customs followed in the burial of an Egyptian king, the earthly representative of the great Ancient Egyptian God, Ra.

The sight alone is overpowering and the imagination can hardly carry us within the sarcophagus, for there, when its lid is raised – which I hope will be in the course of a few weeks – the contents will solve a problem which has hitherto baffled archaeologists and, for the first time, modern eyes will look upon the undisturbed work of man, executed three thousand years ago in accordance with the customs of then prevailing religion. Our one haunting regret is that Lord Carnarvon was not spared to witness the fruits of his undertaking.

On 18 January the *Lancet* announced that Dr D. E. Derry, Professor of Anatomy at the Government Medical School in Cairo and a well-known anthropologist, had been charged with the examination of the mummy of Tutankhamen.

It also stated that 'calcified ova of bilharzia* have before now been found in mummified kidneys, and that calcification of the arteries seems to have been one of the commonest of diseases in the time of the pharaohs, affecting both young and old. What else the examination may reveal is a matter for intelligent speculation, but nothing is likely to miss the combined efforts of anatomist, anthropologist and radiologist.'

Whereas the world waited on tiptoe to learn the contents of the sarcophagus, Howard Carter and his colleagues were not to be hurried. It took them three weeks to dismantle the first and

* A dread disease of Egypt contracted through a parasite found in stagnant water.

outer shrine. Even the press, ever impatient for news, recognised the professionalism of the archaeologist.

Mr Carter and his associates, however, have a stupendous task before them and, although they are naturally keen about getting to the sarcophagus, they do not intend to hurry operations to the detriment of the scientific interests involved. The restraint and patience they have displayed this season are remarkable, and only equalled by the self-control with which they waited until the antechamber had been completely cleared of its contents, before they pierced the sealed wall which had tantalized their gaze ever since they had first entered the tomb two and a half months previously.

They have, in fact, determined throughout to subordinate their own feelings to the interests of the science which they are serving and to preserve every vestige of the evidence which might prove of use in the compilation of the records of the obscure period to which Tutankhamen belongs.

This was praise indeed.

Luxor was now the focal point of the world's news media. In addition to the legions of newsmen, hundreds upon hundreds of tourists began to flood the little town straddled along the banks of the Nile.

It was at this critical juncture that officialdom decided to flex its muscles. This, no doubt, was occasioned by an understandable jealousy caused by the news media of the world insisting on by-passing the government agencies for the first time under the control of a freely elected Egyptian government, being only intent on speaking directly with the English and American archaeologists. On 12 February the following communique was issued by the Egyptian government:

Tutankhamen's Tomb: Opening of Sarcophagus and Visits to View.

The following arrangements have been decided upon by the Ministry of Public Works.

Photo: 'The Times'

Close-up of the entrance to the tomb, with treasures being carried up the sixteen steps. For centuries tourists had walked above this treasure house; beneath their feet wealth beyond their dreams.

1. The opening of the sarcophagus of Tutankhamen is to be
   carried out on February 12th, 1924, at 3 p.m., in the
   presence of the Under-Secretary of State for Public Works;
   the Mudir of the Province; the Director-General of Antiquities; the Chief Inspector of Antiquities, Upper Egypt;
   the Assistant Conservator of the Museum; the Inspector of
   Antiquities at Luxor; Mr Lucas and Mr Carter, and those
   of his collaborators who are designated by the Under-
   Secretary of State for Public Works and Mr Carter.

2. The press is to be admitted on the morning of February
   13th between 10 a.m. and noon.

3. The following days – viz. 14th, 15th, 16th and 17th -- will
   be devoted to making records by Mr Carter and his staff,
   and the necessary preparations for the reception of authorised visitors.

The Pharaoh's spirit, having moved into the outer firmament among
the circum-polar stars, no longer resides in the Royal Kas. One of the
priceless statues, under Callender's supervision (just visible), is carefully
manœuvred out of the tomb.

Photo: 'The Times'

4. Authorised visitors will be permitted to visit the tomb during ten days, beginning as soon as possible after February 17th. The actual date will depend upon the contents of sarcophagus; this and the procedures to be adopted to obtain permits will be announced in the press as soon as possible.

5. With the exception of February 13th, which is to be devoted to the press view, all visits will be suspended from now until the tomb is opened to authorised visitors.

The last four lines of Clause 1 were revealing and when Carter and Callender read them, the former was only just able to contain his outrage. The writing was already on the wall, or, at least, contained within the statement!

Within the tomb Carter was intent upon finalising the arrangements for lifting the lid of the sarcophagus. Upon closer examination it was found to have been broken, although the crack had been carefully sealed over and painted. Perhaps this was, in fact, a second accident, for one would have expected architects of the calibre of those employed, to have insisted on a quartzite lid, in keeping with the sarcophagus itself.

Callender had now all but completed his preparations for raising the mammoth one and a quarter tons of granite. Great beams of timber stood in place of the outer shrines, and were shored up at either side, butting on to the walls of the chamber. Solid pieces of iron were clamped to the lid and, above, a heavy derrick, with differential gears, had somehow been hung from the cross-timbers. The headroom was virtually nil. The excavators had decided to raise both pieces of granite together. Now all they needed was to attach the ropes and gently take the strain.

Of one thing Howard Carter had been determined; so far as the official ceremony was concerned, his official guest-list would include as many American representatives as he could manage to squeeze in. This was the least he could do in recognition of

The author between Sheik Abd-el-Maaboud, whom Adamson called 'Abdul', and his son. Maaboud is in his seventies and worked for Carter from 1921–29.

the generosity and untiring help that they had contributed, all without the mention of a cent in payment.

Some ten days previously he had gone to Cairo in order to make amicable arrangements for the opening of the sarcophagus. It was agreed with the authorities that, on the opening day, the ceremony should take place in the presence of a representative of the Ministry of Public Works and responsible officials of the Antiquity Service, together with members of Howard Carter's own staff. He had also suggested that leading archaeologists should be invited. Thereafter some hours should be put aside for visits by the press.

Having arrived back at Luxor, Carter received a notification from the government that, outside the government representatives, he could not admit more than twelve people, including his staff. This, the English archaeologist decided, was not only contrary to the arrangements he had made in Cairo, but was a direct insult to the leading archaeologists, whom by now he had already invited and this the government knew. Carter immediately decided to speak to the Under-Secretary of State for Public Works and the said gentleman immediately withdrew the official objection. So far so good.

Howard Carter then explained the fact that, as an act of courtesy to his collaborators, he had invited their wives to also visit the tomb the following morning. However, the matter was not to rest here.

In the valley Adamson and the police were already having difficulty in controlling the crowds.* Once again the guests were foregathering, although on this occasion they were, in the main, eminent archaeologists.

By 3 p.m. the excitement was intense and Carter had again become so nervous that he was almost unable to contain himself. Those present were: the Governor of Keneh Province and Mohamed Zaglûl Pasha (Under-Secretary of State for Public Works); Mr E. S. Harkness (Chairman of the Board of Trustees of the Metropolitan Museum of Art, New York); Dr Breasted (Professor of Egyptology and Oriental History in the University of Chicago), the Chief Inspector of Antiquities, Upper Egypt; Mr A. M. Lythgoe (Curator of the Egyptian Department of the Metropolitan Museum of Art, New York); Professor Newberry (Honorary Reader of Egyptian Art at the Liverpool University); Dr Alan Gardiner, the well-known philologist; Mr H. E. Winlock (Director of the Egyptian Expedition of the Metropolitan Museum of Art, New York); Mr Norman de Garies Davies (of the same museum); Dr Douglas Derry (Professor of Anatomy at the Kasr-el-Aini School of Medicine, Cairo); Mr Robert Mond; M. Foucart (Directeur de l'Institut Français d'Archéologie); M. Bruyère (Directeur de l'Expedition Français); Major the Hon. J. J. Astor; Messrs Mace, Callender, Lucas, Burton and Bethell, and the Assistant Curator of the Cairo Museum.

---

* Between January and March 1924 there were over 12,300 visitors to the tomb and some 270 parties to the laboratory !

Carter glanced around him and nodded to Callender and the slack on the ropes was taken up. Gradually the hemp began to flex and twist as the strain increased. Then the ropes became taut as bowstrings, the block and tackle groaning in the absolute silence. Suddenly, belying its weight, the two pieces of stone rose smoothly from their quartzite bed. Nervously re-positioning one of the lamps Carter and those colleagues nearest him peered in, while the lid gently swayed a foot or two above them. First reactions were slightly anticlimatic for, whatever the contents, it was swathed in a linen shroud. Although slightly faded the material seemed in perfect condition. Hesitating for only a moment and quickly looking around at the expectant faces, Carter began to roll back the material.

As he did so there was an audible, enthralled reaction; some sucking in air between their teeth, one calling upon the Almighty in his first, uncontrolled burst of excitement, while the rest stood struck dumb with the magnificence of the sight that met their gaze.

Merton described it thus.

The shrouds had covered a perfect anthropoid coffin of wood and gesso gilt of colossal size, almost filling the sarcophagus and resting on a low bier, with gilt lion heads superbly modelled at the head. The hands were crossed upon the chest, the right holding the flail, and the left a crook sceptre, both of gold and faience. On either side of the coffin was the figure of a protective goddess, each with arms and wings outsretched across the body, striking a really pathetic note. But it was the head that drew everyone's attention and admiration. The face was one solid piece of gold, with eyes of crystal and, on the forehead, an urœus (sacred serpent) and a vulture of gold faience encircling the latter, being a 'Crown of Justification' made of olive leaves. The face is, indeed, a very remarkably real portrait and, as one looked at it, one forgot for a moment that the human-shape figure before one was merely a coffin and one seemed to be in the

F

A triumphant Howard Carter – walking-stick in hand – leads the escort as a treasure is removed from the tomb. A photographer dances attendance on the boulders alongside the path.

presence of the body of some great person 'lying in state', so lifelike were the features and so perfect was the modelling.

The coffin is a perfectly magnificent sight, far excelling any other known. There before us, a product of the splendid age to which he belonged, lay the coffin of a king whose name has been on everyone's lips for the past year, and the romantic circumstances of the discovery of whose tomb – indeed, romance surrounds every phase of its investigation – will cause him to be remembered when most other episodes have passed from public memory.

And, as we stood gazing into this wonderful casket, the reflection came to us that, while in the world above great empires had arisen and fallen, wars and cataclysms had convulsed the universe, invasions had completely changed the face of the land, civilisations had sprung up, developed and disappeared, religions had come into existence and had been superseded by others, here, beneath the earth within a few inches of where, daily, century upon century, human feet had trodden, unheeded by all the peoples above, forgotten by everyone until but fifteen months ago, had lain this king in the peace and grandeur which only death and the grave can give!

In fact, the face and features of the king were wrought in sheet-gold. The eyes were of aragonite and obsidian, the eye-

The now venerable 'Boss Gaffir' Abd-el-Maaboud photographed by the author, carrying Howard Carter's silver topped walking-stick, presented to him by the archaeologist upon his leaving Egypt for the last time. The author found that this sheik still uses this much prized possession.

brows and eyelids inlaid with lapis lazuli glass. The two emblems, worked in brilliant inlay – the cobra and the vulture – were the traditional symbols of Upper and Lower Egypt, over which this boy-king ruled.

Absorbed within their own thoughts the official guests quietly made their way up the long passage and climbed the steps, to be confronted by the hot afternoon sun and the expectant stares of a thousand eyes peering at them intently from the parapet above.

At this moment of high triumph, humbled by what he had seen, Carter reverently replaced the linen shrouds and walked out into the open air. Unfortunately, at what should have been a moment of exhilarating triumph, he was about to find himself at the epicentre of a political earthquake.

Howard Carter had barely reached the bank of the Nile in front of the Winter Palace Hotel, when he was handed a letter. It read:

S.S. *Missir*, Feb. 12th, 1924

Dear Mr Carter,

I regret to inform you that I have received a telegram from the Minister of Public Works, in which he regrets that the arrangement came to with the Ministry does not permit the admission of the wives of your collaborators to the tomb tomorrow, February 13th.

Yours sincerely,
M. A. Zaghlûl

If this act was not sufficient to incense the heavily committed archaeologist, a message from Adamson was certainly calculated to do so. It was to the effect that the Government had just sent out extra police to reinforce the inspectors in the execution of the order to prevent any lady from entering the tomb. Howard Carter had had enough and immediately consulted his colleagues. He then stormed back to the Winter Palace and posted up the following notice:

Owing to the impossible restrictions and discourtesies on the part of the Public Works Department and its Antiquity Service, all my collaborators, in protest, have refused to work any further upon the scientific investigation of the discovery of the tomb of Tutankhamen. I, therefore, am obliged to make known to the public that immediately after the press view of the tomb this morning, between 10 a.m. and noon, the tomb will be closed and no further work carried out. Signed Howard Carter.

This notice burst like a thunderclap over the far from peaceful scene, exactly as Carter had determined that it should.

The origins of the row went back to an exchange of correspondence that had been taking place since December last, in which Howard Carter had been pressing the rights of his patrons, principally, Almina, countess of Carnarvon. Carter's formal protest to the Government was contained in his letter of 3 February. Part of it read as follows:

Sir, I have the honour to reply to your letter of January 10th, 1924, No. 27/2/5, and I take this opportunity of replying further to your two letters of December 10, Nos. 18/14/4 and 27/2/5, and your letter of December 6, 1923, unnumbered. (In your letter of January 10, 1924, you speak of your letter of December 16, 1923, No. 39/3/32. I have received no such letter and presume that you refer to the letter of December 6, 1923, which was left unnumbered by an oversight.)

I note with regret that you have consulted your State Legal Department. I say with regret, because it appears to me that the more dignified, as well as the more prudent, course would have been to postpone all dispute as to the ultimate destination of the treasures found until the continued existence of the treasures themselves should have been secured.

By Articles 8, 9 and 10 of the Concession granted to Earl Carnarvon on April 18, 1915, and renewed each subsequent year until the death of Lord Carnarvon in April, 1923, it is provided that:

(8) Mummies of the kings, of princes, and of high priests, together with their coffins and sarcophagi, shall remain the property of the Antiquities Service.

(9) Tombs which are discovered intact, together with all the objects which they may contain, shall be handed over to the Museum whole and without division.

(10) In the case of tombs which have already been searched the Antiquities Service shall, over and above the mummies and sarcophagi intended in Article 8, reserve for themselves all objects of capital importance from the point of view of history and archaeology, and shall share the remainder with the permittee. As it is probable that the majority of such tombs as may be discovered will fall within the category of the present Article, it is agreed that the permittee's share shall sufficiently recompense him for the pains and labour of the undertaking.

The tomb of Tutankhamen has been searched. It was not found intact. The conclusions to be drawn from these documents appear to me to be sufficiently obvious.

As you are doubtless aware, I so far have had time to examine but a small part of the contents of the tomb, and the opportunity to examine and make notes on the rest is a fundamental right, which I will not give up, and which I stand ready to protect, if necessary. This right on my part appears to have been clearly recognised by yourself in July 1923, when, 'to put the matter in order' on the death of Earl Carnarvon, you gave to Almina, Countess of Carnarvon, authorisation to complete the work of clearing the tomb of Tutankhamen – the only condition attached to the authorisation referred to was that your Department reserved to itself such right of control as would enable it to avoid the criticisms made by the Press in the previous year, and to protect the workers as far as possible from unnecessary visits.

On the other hand, it was expressly recognised that the right of publication was entirely reserved to the Countess.

At the same time I must inform you that I will not agree to the new form of contract, by which the Government reserves to itself rights which, as you assure me, it does not propose to exercise.

I shall now endeavour to make clear my reasons:

(1) The Ministry claims the right of control of entry of visitors to the tomb. Article 2 of the Concession already referred to provides that the 'work shall be exercised under the control of the Antiquities Service, who shall have the right not only to supervise the work but also to alter the manner of execution if they so deem proper for the success of the undertaking'.

If the proposed control of visitors had anything to do with the success of the undertaking I should be the last to complain. It has not. The greater number of visitors whom I have been compelled to admit have been Press Agents and the object of their admission has been, not to ensure the success of the undertaking, but to encroach upon the right of publication, which, it has been admitted, belongs entirely to Almina, Countess of Carnarvon.

Time has been wasted, not only on unnecessary visits, but also on fruitless discussions. Between October 22, when I started work this season, and December 17, there were 50 working days. Of these I spent 14 on two journeys to Cairo for discussion, one at Kurna in discussion with yourself, and two were devoted to unnecessary visits by Press Agents. Thus a third of the time was frittered away through Departmental interference, and additional demands on your part have caused further and almost equally serious interruptions to our work from that time down to the present moment.

On the other hand, you propose that I should not admit anyone to the tomb when I am working, without a permit from your Department. The suggestion that every time I wish to ask the advice of experts in any branch of the subject which the work may require, I should first have to apply to your Department for permission, is, in my opinion, preposterous. It is conducive not to the success of the undertaking, but to the very opposite result.

(2) The Government claims the right to dictate to me whom I may and whom I may not employ, and insists on my submitting a list of the names of my collaborators. Again, if this claim had anything to do with the success of the undertaking I might hesitate to resist. But it has nothing to do with the success of the undertaking.

You were good enough to state your personal feelings, and I will state mine. The work on which I am engaged is done not for gain, but in the interests of science. The discovery of the tomb has produced great benefits for Egypt and for the Egyptian Antiquities Department in particular. It has also produced rights in the Earl of Carnarvon, the author of those benefits. It is a matter of surprise and regret to me that, whereas every other Department of the Egyptian Government has shown only goodwill, kindness, and eagerness to help, your Department has, ever since the death of the late Lord Carnarvon, not only been endeavouring to frustrate the rights of the Carnarvon family, but also to impede, hinder, and delay the scientific work, without which the fruits of the discovery would be wasted. I am at a loss to find the motives for this action, but I have no doubt as to which will be the verdict of the world of science on the issue between us.

The English archaeologist was not a man to be trifled with. He had suffered the pinpricks of bureaucracy, the demands of the press, the inhibiting attentions of the tourists and now, in the midst of his highly demanding work, he was being baited by officialdom. Four of his most eminent collaborators immediately sent their own letter to *The Times*.

Sir, In reference to the difficulties that have rendered the work in the tomb of Tutankhamen impossible, as was made known to the world today, we, the undersigned, shall be indebted to you if you will give publicity to the accompanying letter which, in the interests of science, we deemed it necessary to address to M. Lacau, Director-General of the Service of Antiquités. This letter will indicate the attitude we were adopting a fortnight ago when we still hoped to avert the catastrophe that has now occurred.

Yours truly,

James H. Breasted,	Director of the Oriental Institute and Professor of Egyptology and Oriental History in the University of Chicago.
Alan H. Gardiner,	sometime Editor of the *Journal of Egyptian Archaeology*.
Albert M. Lythgoe,	Curator of the Egyptian Department of the Metropolitan Museum of Art, New York, and Head of the Museum's Egyptian Expedition.
Percy E. Newberry,	sometime Brunner Professor of Egyptology at the University of Liverpool.

The following is the text of the letter referred to :

Luxor, January 30, 1924

M. Pierre Lacau, Director-General of Antiquities, Cairo.

Dear Monsieur Lacau,

We feel it our duty to science to call your attention, as Director-General of Antiquities, to a very serious condition which is affecting the regular progress of the work in the tomb of Tutankhamen, and which is clearly endangering the scientific record resulting from that work.

That unique discovery, with its wealth of historical and archaeological facts, belongs not to Egypt alone, but to the entire world. The interest which it has aroused has penetrated into all corners of the globe, and has focused upon Egypt an unprecedented degree of attention among men of all classes and professions.

Moreover, it is universally agreed among archaeologists that

Mr Howard Carter is conducting his complex and very difficult task in a manner beyond all praise. Altogether, apart from the collaborators who happen to be among the signers of this letter, it is everywhere recognised that the co-workers assembled by Mr Carter form a group of scientists of unsurpassed ability and experience, such as has never been at the disposition of any other archaeological enterprise in this country before; and you yourself have acknowledged your complete satisfaction with the results they are achieving.

Nevertheless their work has, unfortunately, been interrupted this season, not once, but repeatedly, by the demands which you have brought as to the regulation of visitors and other questions of a similar nature – matters which are undeniably inconsequential in comparison with the security of the scientific record of the tomb and the preservation of its contents.

Besides endangering the completeness and security of the records, the unnecessary delays now being incurred are seriously obstructing and delaying related enterprises of the cooperating staffs. These are irretrievable and totally unnecessary scientific losses of time, ability, and available funds by organisations present in this country to serve science, but in this particular case, accomplishing a vast amount of costly work which accrues chiefly to the benefit of the Egyptian Government without having cost the Government a penny.

We feel obliged, therefore, to put ourselves on record at this time as calling your attention to the serious nature of the present interruptions and to the further fact that unless the unnecessary difficulties now obstructing the work in the tomb of Tutankhamen are moderated we can only hold one opinion – namely, that you, as Director-General of Antiquities, are failing completely to carry out the obligations of your high office to protect the scientific procedure of this all-important task.

It is hardly necessary for us to call attention to the unfortunate effect of such failure of your administration upon the public and the great scientific world now so eagerly following the progress of the task.

Believe us to be, very sincerely yours,

James H. Breasted,

Alan H. Gardiner,

Albert Lythgoe,

Percy E. Newberry

CHAPTER TEN

'DEADLOCK'

THE authorities acted quickly in response to the Howard Carter statement pinned up in the local Luxor hotels. They decided to issue their own public statement, which was published in the local newspapers.

Merton explained the tangled skein in the following despatch to *The Times* on 15 February.

ANOTHER LUXOR SURPRISE
NEW DISCOURTESY
TOMB SHUT AGAINST MR CARTER

There was a further serious development in the Tutankhamen situation this morning, when Mr Carter visited the Valley of the Kings and found that the Government staff on duty there had orders to refuse him admission.

Ibrahim Effendi, the Inspector of Antiquities at Luxor, produced an 'ordre de service' which he handed to Mr Carter. Except that it was in French, it was substantially as follows:

Luxor, February 13, 1924. The Tomb of Tutankhamen is closed until further orders, and neither Mr Carter nor his collaborators, nor any member of the Service, nor any other persons are permitted to enter. This applies both to the Tomb of Tutankhamen and Number 15, serving as laboratory. In case of any unusual event taking place, immediate notification is to be sent by telephone to the Chief Inspector of Antiquities at Luxor, and to the Mamur, the latter to inform the Mudir of Kench. The Chief Inspector of Antiquities will be in charge.

Mr Carter asked if he might have a copy of the order since he had never seen it. Ibrahim Effendi said he was unable to give it without the permission of the Chief Inspector.

In his despatch Merton further explained:

There are several points which require to be made clear. In an interview reported in the local press the Minister of Public Works states that Mr Carter, when in Cairo a week ago, requested that the wives of his collaborators should be admitted, and the Minister refused. This statement is untrue, as no reference to this matter was made in the Cairo interview.

The Government claims that it was compelled by Mr Carter's action in shutting down the tomb to place an armed force in the Valley. I can but repeat the statement already telegraphed, that this force, which was sent to the Valley on Wednesday for the express purpose of preventing the ladies from entering the tomb, was ordered out before the Government had any idea of what Mr Carter's attitude towards its order would be.

The Government, further, is trying to make out that Wednesday's incident is the sole cause of the trouble, but the truth is that it was only the culminating point of a series of acts of unwarrantable interference on the part of the Government since the work was resumed in October.

This was Merton's reasonably objective assessment of the situation.

Egypt seethed with accusation and counter-accusation.

Archaeologists of all nationalities firmly backed Howard Carter, while the government and government-controlled press were vitriolic in their campaign against Carter. It was obvious that the incident had been seized upon as an ideal opportunity to pour out anti-British propaganda. There was a minor, if more humorous incident. The special police guard sent to the valley with orders to keep Carter out of the tomb, sought shelter in the tent which Carter, himself, had lent the police at the beginning of the season. The government had failed to provide them with either shelter, water or fuel – all of which Howard Carter supplied at his own expense! But there were faults on both sides.

The prohibition to enter the laboratory was likely to have a disastrous effect. Among the objects undergoing treatment was the pall, which had only been partially preserved and was lying out in the open, covered merely by a linen sheet. This was adequate for overnight protection, but not for long periods, such as it was now passing through.

Although Howard Carter had shut down the work as a protest against the attitude of the government, it should have been possible for him to carry out the necessary precautionary measures to save this pall and other treasures only partially preserved. On the other hand, it was ridiculously stubborn of the Antiquities Department and government not to allow the experts, sitting in the valley twiddling their thumbs, to take steps to protect these items. The Times newspaper was also caught up in the furore to such an extent that, at the height of the battle, the directors deemed it necessary to issue a statement on their own behalf.

Rather more than a year ago, The Times was approached by the late Lord Carnarvon, and subsequently by Mr Howard Carter, with the request that it should relieve them of this task (the distribution of the official news and photographs), which was becoming too great a tax on their own time and energies, and greatly hampered their proper work as explorers.

There was never any question of securing special advantage for The Times, which accepted the work on the understanding that the news and photographs thus obtained should be available, at a price estimated to cover the cost, to any newspaper in the world which desired to print them.

They have, in fact, been so provided and published simultaneously with *The Times* by nearly all the leading newspapers, many of which have testified to their complete satisfaction with the arrangement. The Egyptian newspapers, by a special concession, have been supplied with the service free of charge.

No profit has accrued to *The Times* from the transaction,

The discoverers and their staff at the entrance to the tomb of Rameses IX some few feet above the resting place of Tutankhamen *From left to right:* Arthur Mace, Hon. Richard Bethell, A. R. Callender, a lady, Howard Carter, Lord Carnarvon, A. Lucas and Harry Burton. None of these persons are alive in 1972, fifty years after the discovery.

Photo: 'The Times'

which cannot by any stretch of imagination be held to constitute a monopoly.

The bemused archaeologists were next accorded the doubtful distinction of attracting the attention of the Prime Minister at a tea-party. Zaghlul Pasha declared that his government was determined to maintain its attitude, 'Because it was right

Crated treasures on the little trucks of the Décauville railway, for transportation from the Valley of the Kings to the waiting barges on the Nile.

and because it must safeguard its dignity and country's interests.'

But, happily, there were signs that each side was endeavouring to find a compromise while, at the same time, the government began to consider what steps to take if Howard Carter refused any proposals put to him. The Antiquities Department let it be known that, in such an event, they themselves would take possession of the tomb and carry on work with their own staff.

However, the newspaper, *Egyptian Gazette*, stated emphatically: 'The task would be an impossible one for the Government, which has not in its employ a single official competent to undertake this work.'

This last statement sounds sweeping, so it is as well to point out that it represented the unanimous view of all the eminent Egyptologists currently at Luxor.

On 20 February the government acted. An order of the Ministry of Public Works, signed that afternoon, stated:

Considering that on February 13th Mr Howard Carter interrupted the execution of the programme of work agreed to, by closing down the tomb and publicly declaring that further work was impossible, and, when on February 18th he was formally invited to resume work, he declined, and proposed unjustifiable and unacceptable conditions;

Considering that the abandonment of the work and the closing of the tomb constitute a grave infraction of Mr Carter's obligations; and

Considering that Article 13 of the Authorisation of 1915 empowers the Government to cancel the contract by reason of any infraction by the permittee, and seeing that the cancellation is all the more urgent because Mr Carter, in his letter of February 3rd, denied the Government rights in the antiquities discovered;

Therefore, Mr Carter's authority for excavation is declared to be cancelled, and the Director-General of Antiquities is ordered to re-open the tomb and resume work at the earliest possible moment.

Howard Carter reacted swiftly and decided to apply to the Mixed Courts for a writ restraining the Egyptian government from entering the tomb. The application was to be heard on the Saturday. Carter also instituted a second lawsuit in the Civil Chamber of the Mixed Courts, asking for an order against the Minister of Public Works to allow him (Mr. Carter) to enter the tomb and resume work and share equally the discoveries, in accordance with Article 11 of the Antiquities Ordinance.

On 21 February, Pierre Lacau, Director-General of Antiquities, sent a telegram to Howard Carter informing him of his intention to begin the re-opening of the tomb at 2 p.m. on Friday. He invited Howard Carter to be present, in order to give 'information which would help in the work of the conservation of the contents of the tomb'.

Lacau's first task would be to secure, in some measure, the granite lid of the sarcophagus which still hung perilously by its ropes and tackle.

On 21 February the Prime Minister gave an official interview and was quoted as follows:

> Not at any moment has our action been influenced by Mr Carter's nationality. On the contrary, because of that nationality and our sincere desire that nothing should happen to trouble the friendly relations between the two countries, the Egyptian Government has never ceased to display much consideration and quite special sympathy for Mr Carter, and I can assure you that if the Concession-holder had been an Egyptian, we would not have treated him with as much consideration.
>
> Unfortunately the Government's conciliatory attitude was not appreciated by Mr Carter, who compelled us by his conduct to apply the regulations, but not before we had shown in regard to him, for science's sake, much patience. I think that in England, as everywhere else, it is the duty of the Government to defend the right and dignity of the nation. That is what we have done and our attitude has not been dictated by any other consideration.
>
> It has been alleged that our action was taken with the view to pleasing the public. This is not correct. We could not allow an infringement of our rights, nor permit the Government's authority and agreements to be disregarded. But supposing we had taken into consideration the sentiment of the Egyptian public, I see no harm in that, especially since, in the present instance, this sentiment is in conformity with right. We have, therefore, a double reason for respecting it.

Photo: 'The Times'

As the barges were unable to get closer to the bank, the treasures had to be man-handled across the shallows of the Nile.

Besides, I do not consider that a constitutional Government can disregard the opinion of the country.

It was indeed fortunate that, at this high point of the dispute, rumour had it that the Minister of Public Works was prepared to grant a new concession to Almina, countess of Carnarvon, which was to be drawn up in precise terms, allowing no doubt of its interpretation. It appeared that the Egyptian government, having stood for its dignity in the face of compelling circumstances, was now prepared to seek a peaceful solution.

This was reported on good authority by Reuters.

However, in spite of this, the following morning M. Pierre Lacau, Director-General of the Antiquities Service, sent a letter to Howard Carter demanding the keys of the tomb.

After due consideration by his advisers, the archaeologist replied that, as an action was being heard in the courts the following day, it would be wrong for him to hand them over.

Not to be outdone, at two-thirty that afternoon, Lacau, accompanied by the Mudir, the Chief of Police, the Chief Inspector of Antiquities and a police escort, forced the doors of Tutankhamen's tomb and those of the laboratory. This they did by filing through the eyes of the locks securing the outer wooden doors and then severing the chains securing the steel inner doors.

Adamson had been instructed by Carter not to obstruct them in their task. When they entered the sepulchre chamber it was fortunate that they found the lid of the sarcophagus still suspended in position. After much thought they laid planks across the top of the sarcophagus and lowered the lid to rest upon them. Having completed the task they secured the doors with new padlocks and left the tomb under heavy police and military guard. Adamson also remained on site.

On 24 February, in Cairo, legal proceedings began and the Referee Court had before it an application from Howard Carter and the three executors of the will of the late Lord Carnarvon to be nominated as sequesters of Tutankhamen's tomb.

The plaintiffs were represented by F. M. Maxwell, while the Egyptian government employed a member of the legal department of the Ministry of Public Works.

Meanwhile, it was announced that a new official opening of the tomb would be conducted by the government, which would be honoured by a visit of the Prime Minister and his entire cabinet, together with members of the diplomatic corps.

On 29 February Howard Carter withdrew his action against the Egyptian government and a new action was substituted in the name of Almina, Lady Carnarvon, and General Sir John Maxwell, one of Lord Carnarvon's executors.

However, behind the scenes great efforts were being made to try and settle the dispute amicably and the American achaeologist, James Breasted, agreed to act as a mediator on behalf of the countess of Carnarvon and Howard Carter.

At six o'clock on 5 March 1924, the first of several special trains pulled out of Cairo Station, bearing ministers and members of the Wafd Party and members of both Houses of Parliament on the first stage of their visit to the Valley of the Kings. The station and platform were thronged with crowds of Zaghlûlist supporters who cheered and screamed their devotion to their leader who, unfortunately, was unable to be present himself owing to an indisposition.

At Luxor similar scenes occurred and the Winter Palace Hotel was surrounded by vast crowds of joyful and patriotic Egyptians. In spite of the fact that Lord and Lady Allenby also attended, all the archaeologists, both British and American, decided to boycott the occasion and they were conspicuous by their absence.

On 12 March the referee of the Mixed Tribunals in Cairo, Judge Crabites, found, on all legal points, in favour of the applicants and adjourned the case for the parties to appear in person before him to discuss what was to be done. This was, indeed, a sweet victory for Howard Carter and the executors of the Carnarvon estate who, it was agreed in court, had already invested almost fifty thousand pounds.

However, during the action General Maxwell had, on behalf of the Carnarvon estate, made a generous offer which he confirmed in a letter to the Minister of Public Works.

Dear Minister,

In order to put an end to an acrimonious dispute and to restore the peaceful relations indispensable for future scientific work in Egypt and, in particular, to enable Mr Howard Carter to complete the invaluable work he has begun, I hereby voluntarily relinquish all claims on the part of Almina, countess of Carnarvon and the trustees and executors of the estate of the late Lord Carnarvon to the antiquities in the tomb of Tutankhamen, and agree to withdraw all legal actions, as far as they relate to the enforcement of such claim.

At the same time I would invite the attention of the Egyptian government to the enormous value of the discovery to Egypt, to the expense of the costly work of salvage in the tomb already incurred and still to continue, all of which accrues to the benefit of the Egyptian Museum and the Egyptian government and people, without cost to them. The Egyptian government has repeatedly recognised that, in the work of salvaging the incomparable monuments of which he was the discoverer, Mr Carter has shown untiring devotion and an efficiency beyond all praise, while his staff have likewise rendered invaluable service in the same task. Under these circumstances I venture to mention that there are a large number of duplicate objects in the tomb, and to call attention to the appropriateness of recognition of the above services to the Egyptian government by the presentation of some of those duplicates to the British Museum and the Metropolitan Museum, New York, in the name of the countess of Carnarvon.

The end result of this letter was that the Minister of Public Works adamantly refused to discuss any terms of settlement.

Fortunately, behind the scenes, other and potentially more fruitful negotiations were still in progress, until suddenly the government decided to appeal against the court ruling.

On 19 March the appeal came before Judge Eeman at the Mixed Courts at Alexandria. The government lawyer immediately attacked Howard Carter and Lord Carnarvon for, as he alleged, 'commercialising' the discovery and insisted that the tomb of Tutankhamen was a state domain and that the government's concellation of the concession and entry into the tomb were administrative acts which did not come within the jurisdiction of the Mixed Courts.

The case was adjourned until 29 March to permit the Procureur-General to intervene. Rightly or wrongly, Howard Carter decided to waste no more time locally and, two days later, left Cairo *en route* for London via Venice.

Ten days later the Mixed Court of Appeal at Alexandria gave judgment in favour of the Egyptian government against the referee's decision. Howard Carter heard the news in England and was bitterly disappointed.

On his return to England the discoverer of the tomb found himself, unaccustomedly, in the role of a national hero. The experience was bittersweet; a hero on one hand, while on the other, his academic sensibilities outraged.

He knew that, in Luxor, the air and humidity must already be attacking those many priceless objects, both in the laboratory and in the tomb. Would they withstand the assault? What lay beneath that glittering coffin? Without doubt, there were a thousand answers to a thousand academic questions which, even now, he was being forced to abandon. His frustration and demoralisation was complete. Nevertheless, behind the scenes, his friends were still hard at work.

Even the rector of the City church of St Anne and St Agnes, Bishop Bury, entered upon the controversy from his pulpit. He hazarded the somewhat obvious reaction that 'the world was waiting for the actual unwrapping of the mummy' and that this would be 'the greatest archaeological event in modern history'. He further suggested that to leave the tomb as it was 'would be a constant temptation to all the tomb robbers of Egypt; more especially dangerous now that Egypt was free from British control'! He further added that 'he could not help thinking that, in time, feelings would die down and that Mr Carter would return. How could anyone else be asked to finish the great work? Such a solution was unthinkable. It was perhaps to be regretted that there should have been a decision to 'down tools'. It was easy to be wise after the event but, personally, he would not have gone 'on strike'. He thought that that was a great mistake. 'To go off and leave the tomb gave the opportunity to authority to go in and break the seals. It would have been better to have said: "If you will not allow in the wives of my colleagues then I will not allow anyone else to come in." After all, it was Mr Carter's tomb; he had his concession and to have stayed in possession would have been better. To dispossess him would have meant a long legal action. At the same time, he desired to make it understood that he was not judging Mr Howard Carter!'

The bishop rounded off his personal appraisal with the thought that the difficulties would be forgotten; that there was already a tendency to say that a great deal of fuss had been made about nothing. All the responsible Egyptians, with whom he had conversed, were in agreement that it would be a monstrous thing to displace Mr Carter, and Egyptian journals were impressed by the support given to Mr Carter in all English newspapers.

Bishop Bury proved right. On 12 January 1925, over one year since the dispute had begun and nine months after the closing of the tomb, it was announced that the dispute had been settled. Both sides had backed down from their intransigent positions and it was reported that the settlement had been both amicable and satisfactory to both sides.

The following day Howard Carter exchanged letters with Mohamed Bey Sidky, the Minister of Public Works, which gave him a concession to cover the present and next digging seasons, ending October 1926. The terms of the new agreement provided that the ownership of all objects found would be vested in the Egyptian government, which reserved to itself the absolute discretion to give to Howard Carter, for scientific purposes, such duplicate objects as it might select.

Although no publicity was given to the fact, the negotiators had already obtained from the Egyptian government tacit acceptance that, in exchange for the abandonment of all their claims, the trustees and executors of the Carnarvon estate might reasonably expect recompense for their investment to date.

Throughout all the months of haggling one point had been beyond dispute on both sides, namely, the highly proficient and

professional skill of Howard Carter. For a very short period the
Egyptians had, indeed, tried to take over where he had left off,
but with disastrous results. They then had the wisdom to leave
well alone.

Upon the official signing of the documents Howard Carter
hurried to the Cairo Museum, where the first consignment of
crates lay waiting, untouched; a very sensible and laudable
decision on the part of the authorities. In a new spirit of friendship he and members of the Antiquities Department began the
task of unpacking. It was to find that the objects, including the
Royal Kas, had arrived in perfect condition and were so preserved that they were immediately ready to be placed on public
view.

Throughout this time Adamson, with short absences to relieve
the unbridled monotony, had remained stoically on duty, watching over his master's interest. The world of the popular press
breathed again; correspondents were despatched from all capitals
of the world and Howard Carter left once more for Luxor.

The re-opening of the tomb was in striking contrast to those
many occasions beforehand. The ceremony was simple. Callender had arranged to re-excavate the steps, filled in by the
government after their official re-opening, and, at ten o'clock
on the morning of 25 January 1925, in the presence of representatives of the government, Howard Carter was handed back
the keys.

There was one archaeological disaster. The pall which had
covered the second shrine, in itself a unique fabric and which
Professor and Mrs Newberry had been fighting to preserve, had
been left out in the open, in front of the tomb of Seti II. It had
been inadequately covered and Carter was aghast to find that
it was completely ruined. The Antiquities Department had
taken the necessary steps to safeguard the contents of the tomb,
but had not provided proper protection against exposure to the
sun and air for this priceless relic. No other example of it
exists.

If the press of the world were awaiting Howard Carter to

proceed with the lifting of the coffins from the sarcophagus, they were due for acute disappointment. Already the high heat of summer was scorching the cliffs and chasms of the Royal Valley of the Kings and Carter was not to be rushed.

CHAPTER ELEVEN

TUTANKHAMEN

A T last the summer had spent itself although, even in the first weeks of October 1925, the range of temperature in the valley was anything from ninety-seven degrees to a hundred and five degrees Fahrenheit.

Now that the last and greatest prize of all, the exhumation of the royal mummy itself, was within their grasp, Carter was determined to do all possible to maintain cordial relations with the Egyptian government officials. Believing that they were on the threshold of this revelation, Carter sent a message to the Director-General of the Department of Antiquities, M. Lacau, asking if he would wish to be present at the ceremony, or would be happy to delegate his authority to his assistant. He was abroad at the time, but replied, in due course, that he would wish to be present himself. Yet another delay.

Carter had arranged that the body of the king should first be examined by Dr Douglas Derry, Professor of Anatomy at the Medical School at Kasr-el-Aini, and Dr Saleh Bey Hamdi, formerly director of the same school. Due to the postponement until 10 November, he suggested that they defer their visit.

By now everyone was working with a high degree of cooperation amid much optimism, laced with general excitement and expectation. It was already well over two years since the discovery of the tomb and, as they re-entered the inner chambers, Carter mentally congratulated himself on the precautions he had taken before leaving. He had doused each of the chambers with a variety of insecticides. He had also arranged to cover the sarcophagus with an additional pall. The Turkish oak beams, interlaced with soft deal boards, which had been placed at the entrance to maintain a water-seal in the event of a flood, had effectively created dust-free conditions.

Again the excavators found themselves looking down at the great gilded coffin, which measured an astonishing seven feet four inches in length, was anthropoid in shape, and bore the Khat head-dress. Upon either side of the coffin were two solid silver handles. The question that presented itself for solution was whether these handles, after three thousand years, were robust enough to take the weight of the lid of the coffin. There was only a gap of an inch or two on either side, between the coffin and the side of the quartzite sarcophagus and, in addition to the handles, they found that the shell was fixed to the body of the coffin by ten solid silver tongues, four on each side and one at the head and the foot. These were secured by gold-headed silver pins which the excavators decided could safely be withdrawn, if they could find a method to do so in the strictly confined space.

Additional hoists and tackle were suspended from the cross-beams and attached to the handles. At a word from Carter, Callender gradually began to take the strain on the ropes and, with barely a shudder, the exquisitely worked lid rose solemnly from out of the sarcophagus. All eyes focused within. To everyone's amazement there, beneath it, lay another magnificent, anthropoid coffin. However this one was shrouded in delicate linen, sewn into position, revealing beneath its gossamer fragility the glitter of gold and the outline figure of the young boy-king. This was yet another coffin.

Not a sound could be heard in the chamber as Carter and his friends looked down. Loving hands had again placed floral tributes and olive and willow leaves, cornflowers and the petals of blue lotus upon the human-form casket. A little wreath lay delicately placed upon the forehead.

Unfortunately they could proceed no further as Harry Burton

had not yet arrived back in the valley and, therefore, it was not until 15 October that further progress could be made, after he had completed his photographic record, upon which Howard Carter rightly insisted. This time-lapse enabled the excavators to consider in very great detail how they might remove the nest of exquisite coffins.

They also had time to speculate! Surely, beneath this next lid, must lie the mummy of the king. But one point puzzled them greatly; neither coffin would react with the slightest movement, however much pressure they dared put upon them. If they were not secured one to the other, which seemed extremely unlikely, then they must, of necessity, be supporting a tremendous weight. This seemed puzzling as they, themselves, were only constructed of wood.

Howard Carter now had to consider whether or not both coffins had the tactile strength to withstand a direct lift from out of the sarcophagus. It was an absorbing situation and, from time to time, Adamson could not resist leaving his post above ground to watch and contemplate upon the problems facing the excavators. Owing to the fact that there was not even sufficient room to place a small human hand between the quartzite of the sarcophagus and the outer coffin, they deemed that the only way possible to secure a direct lift was to insert steel pins into the wood of the outer shell and, on to them, secure loops for lifting. To these pins they duly attached pulleys and, some two days after removing the first lid, they began to hoist the two coffins. With nerves at breaking point, the archaeologists watched in agonised silence as, inch by inch, the double coffins emerged from the great block of quartzite.

Twenty minutes later there was just sufficient room to pass substantial oak planks beneath the coffins to straddle the lips of the sarcophagus. They were safe. Now they were able to observe the six feet eight inches of the second coffin in close-up detail. Its workmanship was superb, breathtaking, with magnificent inlay into thick gold foil. This consisted of cut and engraved opaque glass, lapis lazuli and turquoise. Again it symbolised

Osiris, but this time was protected by the exquisite form of the vulture, Nekhebet, and the servant, Buto.

The next problem took another two days to solve. How, with no headroom and no fixing points on the inner, second coffin and not sufficient room to insert steel pins, could they raise the one from the other? The second coffin bore signs of greater fragility and there was evidence of slight decomposition of the wood by moisture. The idea was struck upon that, by the use of the silver pins that had secured the lid, the inner coffin could be supported with copper wires and eyelets, while the outer coffin could then be re-lowered back into the sarcophagus, leaving the second suspended in mid-air. This would also have the advantage of remaining motionless, causing no sudden or undue pressure to be placed upon it.

Again, in an agony of apprehension, the pulleys squeaked and the ropes twisted and flexed with the enormous strain. Gradually the outer coffin returned solemnly to its resting place, while the oak planks were re-inserted to take the weight of the second coffin, under which was placed a veritable bed of cotton wool. So far, so good. Now came the task of raising the lid of the second coffin. This time there was no other method but to insert four steel eyelets in the most unobtrusive positions, upon which to fix the block and tackle. Surely, now, they might be blessed with a view of the king?

This time the lid was less inclined to part company with the main shell of the coffin but, finally, after some heart-stopping moments, it smoothly swung clear and ascended to the roof of the tomb.

Again, like excited schoolboys, the excavators swung the arc-lamps into position and peered inside. To their amazement, yet another coffin, Osirede in form, lay nestling on its bed but, on this occasion, completely hidden by an ochre-coloured shroud, which extended right up to the neck. But here, in unbelievable majesty and beauty, they observed the lifelike features of Tutankhamen executed in burnished gold. With the shroud covering his body it looked, for all the world, as if they were gazing at the dead king's features, newly departed for reasons as yet unknown. They found themselves speaking in muted whispers as Harry Burton again recorded their achievement with solemn professionalism.

When Burton had finished, Howard Carter, with trembling fingers, delicately began to disrobe the form of the king. It was as his fingers came into contact with the cold and smooth metallic surface beneath the linen that he realised, in a rush of awe-inspired incredulity, that the third coffin, which would take eight men to carry it, had been constructed of gold. He turned to his colleagues, his lips, unbelieving, forming the words: 'It's gold . . . solid gold!'

As if mesmerised he continued to remove the shroud, to reveal a sight of such magnificence that mortal eyes had not beholden for three thousand years. The outer measurement of this incredible work of art was six feet one and three-quarter inches which, when the coffin was eventually weighed, turned the scales at two thousand four hundred and forty-eight pounds of pure gold.

But now, on cursory examination, it appeared that a tragedy awaited them. It seemed that, at the funeral ceremonies, vast quantities of a black, lustrous unguent had been poured over the third coffin, not only disfiguring it, but also sticking it hard and fast to the second. The material had a resinous, pitch-like appearance that at first defied any kind of solvent. It was decided that this problem would have to await the attention of the chemists in the laboratory.

Upon closer examination, Carter perceived that the dividing line of the lid and main body of the coffin was free of the unguent and could be lifted at the appropriate time. The top was secured by eight gold tenons, in turn held fast by eight gold nails. These, in due course, were prized from their sockets, leaving the lid free to be raised by the handles fashioned to perfection by the ancient goldsmiths.

For those present, the next few moments were to be the crowning point of a lifetime spent in archaeology. Never again

G

would they savour of such a discovery. Indeed, perhaps no men would ever again be privileged to share in such a unique experience.

Having removed the coffin to the antechamber, they lifted the lid. There before them, in simple dignity, neatly and meticulously laid to rest, was the cocooned mummy-form of the king, but it was to his head that their eyes inevitably became riveted.

There, staring up at the ceiling of the rock-hewn tomb, impassive and tranquil at his dreadful fate, was a magnificent, burnished gold mask, depicting the assured solemnity of a young boy-king, destined, by the great Lord Ra, to enthral and inspire all those who would ever come to gaze upon his features throughout eternity.

CHAPTER TWELVE

EPILOGUE

LUXOR, 13 November 1925. Reuters report that the mummy of the pharaoh, Tutankhamen, was taken out of its wrappings today.

The body was found covered with gold, with stars of gold on the heart and lungs. A large golden dagger was with the body. It is expected that an official communiqué will be published tomorrow.

In fact, it was 17 November before the ministry of public works published the following communiqué:

The examination of the mummy of the pharaoh, Tutankhamen, was continued on the 14th and 15th, when a large number of amulets and jewellery was disclosed, there being as many as sixteen layers on some parts of the body. Among the important objects discovered were two groups of finger rings, altogether thirteen in number, and some twenty bracelets.

The whole chest is covered with magnificently encrusted gold pectorals, two of which form the vulture (Nekhebet) of the kingdom of Upper Egypt, and the Uraeus (Buto), the symbol of Lower Egypt. Beneath these were smaller, but even more beautiful, pectorals of intricate design, including winged scarabs and sacred eyes, and also a marvellous flying vulture, which is an example of the finest goldsmith's craft. This is encrusted with lapis lazuli and cornelian and resembles, in its refined taste, the jewellery of the Middle Empire.

THE LAST PORTRAIT OF TUTANKHAMEN

The Golden mask of Tutankhamen was X-rayed in the Musee du Petit Palais, Paris, whilst some of the treasures were on exhibition for the very first time in Europe.

The purpose of this investigation was not to uncover some hidden object – the mask being hollow – but to examine the mould of the mask which is invisible to the naked eye, and to obtain by means of this experiment a unique portrait of this celebrated head. So now we have a new portrait of the Pharaoh, without volume, without colour, without matter – there remains only the purity of line itself. Although the working of the gold is of admirable regularity throughout, the radio-graph reveals irregularities in the layer of gold on one of the cheeks – (when the Mummy was examined by Howard Carter a scar was found on the cheek). It also confirms that the face and the front and back of the headpiece were formed separately and then joined together by simple hammering of the gold plates. The beard is held in a sleeve which in turn is held on to a protrusion of the chin. One strange feature: since the eyebrows of lapis-lazuli and the eye make-up are applied to the gold, they should appear white or light grey, as does anything which increases the thickness; but, in fact, they appear dark grey on the portrait – another mystery of the tomb which extends to the applied sciences.

The body of the king, which is in a very bad state of pre-servation, affords sufficient evidence for Doctors Derry and Saleh Bey Hamdi to declare his age to have been about eighteen years. Up to the present, the king's head, which is still covered by the gold mask, has not been examined, but this examina-tion will be carried out within the next few days.

The long, anatomical report produced one startling feature, which was seized upon by the press of the world. It appears under the sub-heading:

General Appearance of Head

The head appears to be clean-shaved and the skin of the scalp is covered by a whitish substance, probably of the nature of fatty acid. Two abrasions on the skin covering the upper part of the occipital bone had probably been caused by the pressure of the diadem, which was enclosed by the tightly-wound head bandages. The plugs filling the nostrils and the material laying over the eyes were found by Mr Lucas to consist of some woven fabric, impregnated with resin. Mr Lucas also examined some whitish spots on the skin above the upper part of the back and shoulders, and these proved to be composed of 'common salt with a small admixture of sodium sulphate'. In all probability derived from the natron used in the embalming process. The eyes are partly open and had not been interfered with in any way. The eyelashes are very long. The cartilaginous portion of the nose had become partially flattened by the pressure of the bandages. The upper lip is slightly elevated, revealing the large, central, incisor teeth. The ears are small and well-made. The lobes of the ears are perforated by a circular hole measuring seven point five milli-metres in diameter.

The skin of the face is of a greyish colour and is very cracked and brittle. On the left cheek, just in front of the lobe of the ear, is a rounded depression, the skin filling it, resembling a scab. Round the circumference of the depression, which has slightly raised edges, the skin is discoloured.

This scab approximated to the same position as that in which the mosquito stung Lord Carnarvon and which resulted in his blood-poisoning. From now on the superstitious fever of the curse of the pharaohs knew no bounds and would never abate. The words of the dying Lord Carnarvon were recalled: 'It is finished. I have heard the call and am prepared.'

It had been at this moment that the lights had gone out in Cairo.

From now on anyone who was faintly connected with the excavation of Tutankhamen and who had the temerity to die, received the label of 'another curse victim'. But the list was substantial.

In 1926 Sir William Garstin died at the age of seventy-four, through nothing more unusual than natural old age. But in 1928, Arthur Mace, who had supported Carter so generously, died of tuberculosis at the age of forty-nine. In 1929, the Honourable Richard Bethell, who had acted as Carter's secretary, died suddenly, followed not many months later by the tragic death of his father, the seventy-eight-year-old peer, Lord Westbury. It was upon the latter's hand that Cheiro had also seen the tell-tale sign of suicide.

Universal News Service issued the following report in February, 1930:

> Death of another distinguished person was linked with 'the curse of the pharaohs' today, when Lord Westbury committed suicide. Lord Westbury's son, Richard Bethell, acted as secretary to Howard Carter when the latter supervised the opening of Tutankhamen's tomb at Luxor.
>
> The seventy-eight-year-old peer took his life in a leap from the window of his seventh storey apartment in the fashionable St James's Court, Westminster, crashing through a glass verandah and dying instantly as he struck the pavement.
>
> Lord Westbury had been worried by the death of his son, which occurred suddenly last November. Rumour attributed young Bethell's death to the superstition which declares that

those who violate the tomb of a pharaoh will come to a violent end.

Lord Westbury was frequently heard to mutter, 'the curse of the pharaohs', as though this had preyed on his mind. In a last letter he wrote: 'I cannot stand the horror any longer and I am going to make my exit.'

Also in 1930, the Honourable Mervyn Herbert, half-brother to the present Lord Carnarvon, died at the age of forty-one. In 1932, Sir Charles Cust died at the age of fifty-nine. In 1934, Albert Lythgoe died of arterio-sclerosis.'

The newspapers of the world claimed many more victims, but without the slightest reason to do so. First, there was George J. Gould, a friend of Lord Carnarvon's, who was travelling in Egypt for his health. He was ill long before he visited the country. Then there was the sporting companion of Lord Carnarvon, Woolf Joel; then Sir Archibald Douglas Reid, the X-ray expert, who was going to the tomb to X-ray the mummy, but was destined not to arrive. Another X-ray expert, Frederick Raleigh, also died before reaching the tomb. Arthur Weigall, one-time antiquities inspector and writer of popular books who did, in fact, visit the tomb, but took no part in the excavation. There was Colonel Aubrey Herbert, who never visited the tomb, but perhaps was confused with his brother, Mervyn. Professor Lafleur, of Mcgill University, visited Egypt for his health; he had long been ill. Then there was H. G. Evelyn White, who only visited Egypt before the tomb was discovered. Next, George Benedite arrived after the tomb had been closed for the summer. He never entered it. Professor Casanova may possibly have visited the tomb, but if so, only in the capacity of a tourist. Prince 'Ali Fahmy Bey', who was murdered in the Savoy Hotel in London by his French-born wife. If he was ever in the tomb it was only as a tourist. Then there was a boy run over by Lord Westbury's hearse. Yet again, a workman in the British Museum was said to have fallen dead while labelling objects from the tomb, but in fact the museum had no such objects in its collection.

The legend persists to the present time. In 1966 the Egyptian government agreed to a French proposal to exhibit the treasures of Tutankhamen in Paris. For four months Mohammed Ibraham, Egypt's Director of Antiquities, resisted the arguments of his superiors and of the French ambassador. A few days after he had finally agreed that the treasures might be sent to Paris, his daughter was injured in a motor-car accident and was taken to a Paris hospital in a critical condition. Ibraham then had a dream that he would also meet with a serious mishap. He decided to seek an appointment with the minister of culture in Cairo and beg him to rescind the decision to send the treasures abroad.

On Monday, 19 December 1966, he discussed the matter with French diplomats and was persuaded to ignore all legends of 'the curse', as the Egyptian government had a year earlier closed down all spiritualistic societies in Cairo on the grounds that they were anti-socialist and, at the same time, they officially denounced the legend of the pharaoh's curse as being mere superstition.

As Mohammed Ibraham left this meeting he was knocked down by a car and died two days later of a fractured skull. But the other side of the coin is also impressive.

Richard Adamson slept within the tomb continuously for seven long years and, happily, lives today. The third person to enter the sepulchre chamber, Lady Evelyn Beauchamp, not only survived the malediction, but now lives as a sprightly and charming septuagenarian. Likewise does her brother, the present earl of Carnarvon. However, both of them have had to live a lifetime with the background of the curse constantly brought into sharp focus by journalists the world over. They don't believe in it, or at least hold a neutral position, but when asked if he would re-visit the tomb, the sixth earl of Carnarvon admitted: 'Not for a million pounds!'

What of the young man, the progenitor of the superstition. Certainly, his face portrays no malefic predisposition. Rather it is calm and gentle, with a sweet nobility transcending any such evil intention. Certainly he took no revenge on Howard

Carter himself. He died in March 1939, at the age of sixty-six. His name will also live forever . . . in the annals of dedicated international archaeology.

But what of King Tutankhamen himself? In spite of all the revelations found in his tomb, his life is comparatively obscure. His possible father or brother, Amenophis IV, whose name signified, 'Amun is satisfied', became probably the most profound religious theoretician that Egypt would ever produce. He broke with the priesthood, postulating that there was only one God, Aton, who was represented as a solar disc, from which rays spread out fanwise, terminating in hands.

This signified the sun to be the creative principle of all life, father of all men. Amenophis changed his name to Akhenaton and removed his capital from Thebes, some two hundred and fifty miles to the north, at Tel-el-Amarna, where he practised monotheism for some twenty years.

His wife, Nerfertiti, bore him only daughters. This misfortune may have forced him to marry a concubine who, in turn, could have produced two sons. The eldest, Smenkare, and the youngest, Tutenkhaton. Alternatively, the boys may have been the sons of Amenophis III, and thus brothers or half brothers of Akhenaton. The eldest died at the age of fourteen, but a few months after the death of Akhenaton. The thwarted priesthood of Amun immediately wanted to enthrone their own high priest, Bekanchos, there being no direct male issue.

However, Nerfertiti and her supporters were adamant that Tutenkhaton should inherit the succession. Queen Nerfertiti triumphed and the third of her daughters, Enchesaton, a beautiful child, married Tutenkhaton.

Now erupted a power struggle between the priesthood and the new boy-king, in which the priests of Amun finally triumphed. A 'concordat' or royal decree was issued, stating that the old religion would be re-adopted and that the court would return to Thebes. The young king and his queen changed their names to Tutankhamen and Enchesamun respectively. His reign, at a difficult time in Egyptian history, was undistinguished, but a monumental stone found at Karnak might serve as a justifiable epitaph.

I found the Temple in ruins and the Holy Places partially destroyed. Weeds flourished in its Courts. I restored the sanctuaries and enriched them with costly gifts. I made new images of the gods in gold and adorned them with lapis lazuli and precious stones . . .

The king was twelve at his enthronement and eighteen when he died. Seven short years did he reign. He was a peaceful and studious monarch and it is believed that the couple may possibly have conceived two children, both of whom were stillborn. There was a minstrel who lived in the time of Tutankhamen, named Neferhotep. His words have been handed down through history and perhaps they are a more fitting tribute to Tutankhamen, who graced but a few years on the throne of Egypt.

I have heard those songs that are inscribed in the ancient sepulchres, and what they tell in praise of life on earth and belittling the region of the dead. Yet wherefore do they this in regard to the land of Eternity, the just and the fair, where fear is not? Rangling is its abhorence, nor does any there gird himself against his fellow. That land, free of enemies – in which all our kinsmen from the earliest day of time rest within. The children of millions of millions come thither, everyone. For none may tarry in the land of Egypt; none there is that passeth not thither. The span of our earthly deeds is as a dream. But fair is the welcome that awaits him who has reached the hills of the west.

Now happily, King Tutankhamen, stripped of his treasures, lies sleeping in the tomb plundered by modern man. By the end of 1930 Howard Carter's task was complete. The tomb was empty, except for the quartzite sarcophagus and the mummy of the king.

On 6 June 1930, the Chamber of the Egyptian Parliament adopted the report of its financial commission, recommending the payment of thirty-four thousand, nine hundred and seventy-one Egyptian pounds to the heirs of the late earl of Carnarvon, in reimbursement of the sums spent by him in connection with the discovery of the tomb of the pharaoh, Tutankhamen.

In due time Howard Carter and Richard Adamson came to leave the land of the pharaohs and packed their bags for England. When the ex-military policeman came to shake the sand of the valley from off his feet for the very last time, he had to admit to a rueful smile when he remembered his first conversations with Howard Carter. Was it possible that he had remained there seven long years, when he had vowed not to stop for even seven brief nights.

THE TREASURES OF TUTANKHAMEN

DURING the greater part of 1972 the treasures from the tomb of Pharaoh Tutankhamen will be on display at the British Museum, London. Thereafter they will be found in the Cairo Museum, their permanent resting place.

The mummy of the king lies within a coffin in the quartzite sarcophagus in the Valley of the Kings, Luxor, Upper Egypt, where it may be visited. Information from the Egyptian Tourist Office, Piccadilly, London.